The State of America's Children

DEAR LORD
BE GOOD TO ME
THE SEA IS SO
WIDE AND SO
MY BOAT IS
SO SMALL

Children's Defense Fund

Yearbook 1997

Children's Defense Fund
25 E Street NW
Washington, DC 20001

This book is dedicated to the memories of:

Joseph Cardinal Bernardin,
a man of God who taught us
how to live and how to die,

Robert H. Clampitt,
who gave children a true voice
by founding Children's Express,

Arthur S. Fleming,
a true servant-leader whose long and productive life
furthered the cause of justice for young and old,

Robert Hoderny,
a gifted and dedicated teacher at
Archbishop Carroll High School in Washington, D.C.,
and his 7-year-old foster son, **Kemmie Miller,**
both killed by a car as they crossed a street hand in hand,

Louis Martin,
an incomparable warrior for racial justice,

Rolando Shorey,
who was always there for children in Detroit and never was
afraid to speak out or take risks for them,

and

Ennis Cosby,
a promising young man taken away from
family and friends by the senseless gunfire
that kills a child every hour and a half in America.

Let us honor their memories by our actions
to build a movement to ensure every child
a healthy start in life and safe passage to adulthood.

Acknowledgments

James D. Weill and Donna M. Jablonski oversaw the development of this book and served as editors. Many individuals, at the Children's Defense Fund and elsewhere, contributed to the content and may be contacted for further information about their subjects. At CDF these include: MaryLee Allen and Jamila Larson (Children and Families in Crisis); Helen Blank and Gina Adams (Child Care and Early Education); Stan Dorn and Martha Teitelbaum (Health); Kim Wade (Children, Crime, and Violence); Deborah Weinstein, Arloc Sherman, Nancy Ebb, and Cristina Firvida (Family Income, The New Welfare Law). Data were produced and analyzed by Paul Smith and Janet Simons. Marge duMond copy-edited text, and Janis Johnston managed production.

Special thanks go to contributors from colleague organizations: Nancy Bernstine of the National Housing Law Program (Housing and Homelessness box within the Family Income chapter), Robert Greenstein of the Center on Budget and Policy Priorities (Food and Nutrition), Amy Wilkins and Kati Haycock of the Education Trust (Education), and Susan Wilson of the Network for Family Life Education at Rutgers University (Adolescent Pregnancy Prevention and Youth Development). Clifford M. Johnson, of the Center for Budget and Policy Priorities, provided valuable assistance on youth development issues.

The creation, publication, and distribution of this book were underwritten by an endowment gift from the DeWitt-Wallace Reader's Digest Fund.

Media inquiries should be directed to Sarah Howe.

Contents

Introduction: Standing Strong and Together for Our Children

Speak out for those who cannot speak, for the rights of all the destitute. Speak out, judge righteously, defend the rights of the poor and needy.

Proverbs 31:8-9

Take heed that ye despise not one of these little ones....it is not the will of your Father which is in heaven, that one of these little ones should perish.

Matthew 18:10-14

When we stood, we stood for all of the oppressed people who came before us and generations to come. In our struggle, if we are to bring about the kind of changes that will cause the world to stand up and take notice, we must be committed. There is so much work that needs to be done. Every home and neighborhood in this country needs to be a safe, warm, and healthy place—a place fit for human beings as citizens of the United States. It is a big job, but there is no one better to do it than those who live here. Goodness and change are possible in each and every American citizen. We could show the world how it should be done and how to do it with dignity.

Dr. Martin Luther King Jr.

If a free society cannot help the many who are poor, it cannot save the few who are rich.

John F. Kennedy, Inaugural Speech

Over 3,000 years ago, two slave midwives named Shiphrah and Puah stood up to the king of Egypt, who instructed them, "When you act as midwives to the Hebrew women, and see them on the birthstool, if it is a boy, kill him; but if it is a girl, she shall live." But the midwives feared God and did not do as the king commanded. They let the boys live.

These slave women played unexpectedly significant roles in preventing the annihilation of their people's children and future. Slave midwives would seem powerless. They probably had no intention of becoming social-change agents, revolutionaries, or powerful shapers of history, any more than midwives, mothers, fathers, early childhood educators, child care providers, social workers, nurses, educators, or grandmothers think of themselves as transforming nation-builders and social revolutionaries today.

Yet when Shiphrah and Puah suddenly found that there was no one besides themselves to protect boy children, they ignored the powerful king's order because their respect for God's laws and purposes was stronger than their fear of Pharaoh. They acted for children in the ways available to them. Like many of us, they were probably frightened and overwhelmed by the task and the personal risk. But they were strong and unwavering, cunning and creative in defending the Hebrew children. They had their faith and they had one another. So do we.*

The time comes when each of us must decide: Whom do we fear? Whom will we serve? Whose purposes will govern our actions? What do we stand for? How much are we willing to sacrifice for it? What would happen in America if everyone, or enough of us, in our families, daily work, and communities, determined to make God's order our order, to put our children first, even when it brings us face-to-face with Pharaoh?

If God's concern for children, especially the orphan, the poor, the vulnerable, and the stranger, is to be honored and feared in America and in our world—as the prophets Isaiah, Micah, Jeremiah, Amos, and Ezekiel, and saints Matthew, Luke, Mark, and John taught us—then you and I are

20 Key Facts About American Children

1 in 2	while a preschooler has a mother in the labor force.
1 in 2	lives with a single parent at some point in childhood.
1 in 2	never completes a single year of college.
1 in 3	is born to unmarried parents.
1 in 4	is born poor.
1 in 4	is born to a mother who did not graduate from high school.
1 in 5	is born to a mother who did not receive prenatal care in the first three months of pregnancy.
1 in 5	lives in a family receiving food stamps.
1 in 5	is poor today.
1 in 6	has a foreign-born mother.
1 in 7	has no health insurance.
1 in 7	has a worker in the family but still is poor.
1 in 8	is born to a teen mother.
1 in 8	never graduates from high school.
1 in 9	is born into a family living at less than half the poverty level ($6,079 in 1995).
1 in 12	has a disability.
1 in 14	is born at low birthweight.
1 in 21	is born to a mother who received late or no prenatal care.
1 in 25	lives with neither parent.
1 in 610	will be killed by a gun before age 20.

*The story of Shiphrah and Puah here is inspired by the meditation of Dr. Diana Garland in CDF's *Holding Children in Prayer: A Lenten Guide*.

going to have to join the great cloud of witnesses for righteousness and justice throughout human history in standing up when children are unjustly treated.

If America's children and future are going to be rescued from corrosive and preventable sickness, violence, poverty, ignorance, neglect, and family, moral, and community breakdown, then you are going to have to stand up with me and many others to save them.

If the gaping and growing divisions between Black, Brown, and White, rich and poor, young and old, and men and women are going to be healed rather than widened, then you and I are going to have to stand up and be counted when fairness is tested by politics and inequity is fueled by fear and greed.

America's child, family, and community challenges are legion. But they are solvable, depending on our moral choices as citizens and leaders and on our collective political will. It is unconscionable and unnecessary that an American child drops out of school every eight seconds; is reported neglected or abused every 10 seconds; is arrested

Moments in America for Children

Every 8 seconds	a child drops out of school.
Every 10 seconds	a child is reported abused or neglected.
Every 15 seconds	a child is arrested.
Every 24 seconds	a child is born to an unmarried mother.
Every 34 seconds	a child is born into poverty.
Every 35 seconds	a child is born to a mother who did not graduate from high school.
Every 48 seconds	a child is born without health insurance.
Every minute	a child is born to a teen mother.
Every 2 minutes	a child is born at low birthweight.
Every 3 minutes	a child is born to a mother who received late or no prenatal care.
Every 4 minutes	a child is arrested for drug abuse.
Every 5 minutes	a child is arrested for a violent crime.
Every 5 minutes	a child is arrested for an alcohol-related offense.
Every 17 minutes	an infant dies.
Every 92 minutes	a child is killed by firearms.
Every 2 hours	a child is a homicide victim.
Every 4 hours	a child commits suicide.

every 15 seconds; is born to an unmarried mother every 24 seconds, into poverty every 34 seconds, to a teen mother every minute, and at low birthweight every two minutes; is killed by guns every hour and a half; and commits suicide every four hours.

How do we explain to our children why the richest nation in history lets one in five children grow up poor and lets children be the poorest group of citizens? That a nation that spends $30 million an hour and $22 billion a month on military defense is not powerful enough to protect them from the gun violence that killed 5,751 children in 1993? How do we explain to our children that the world's leader in health technology lets 10 million children go without health coverage even when nine in 10 of them have parents who work?

When will enough of us simply decide as parents, citizens, and people of faith that we have had enough child neglect and suffering, political temporizing and hypocrisy, and draw a moral line in the political sand that no political leader of any party will cross without consequence?

When will the mothers and other women of America stand up to the men in power who control our economic, political, and cultural lives and tell them *we have had enough*—enough of glorifying excessive materialism and violence and sex on our television and movie screens and in our homes, corrupting our children's values and lives?

When will enough religious leaders stand up to enough political leaders and say we will not accept proposals cutting benefits to the poor and weak and young to provide tax breaks to the rich and mighty or proposals to balance the budget that exempt the powerful and ravish the survival assistance of the powerless, young, and poor?

What Does America Believe In?

A colleague pulled from his wallet a frayed *New York Times* clip he has kept since 1968 to remind him why he does what he does. The clip showed a cute, round-faced 9-year-old girl from Concord, N.H., named Holly Harrell, whose faith in the future had been shattered by the deaths of Robert Kennedy and Martin Luther King Jr. When interviewed about her outlook at Christmastime in 1968, she responded, "I don't believe what I used to believe, but I wish I could."

I do too. Don't you wish every one of our children could believe in their parents, teachers, preachers, neighbors, and leaders to protect and provide them a Healthy, Fair, and Moral Start in life and safe passage to adulthood? Don't you wish they believed in themselves, in us, and in our founding creed that "All men [and women and children] are created equal" and "are endowed by their Creator with certain inalienable rights" because they saw it practiced in their daily lives? Don't you wish they and we could believe our political leaders in both parties when they say they will not hurt children and are acting to protect our children's futures rather than their own when they make crucial budget and policy decisions?

Would not many children feel more worthwhile and valuable and less alienated if more adults cared enough about them to protect them, birth to adulthood, from health defects and diseases we could prevent and treat; from neglect and abuse we could alleviate; from corrosive poverty we could eliminate; from ignorance and poor skills good schools could eradicate; from death by guns we could control; from air, water, noise, and cultural pollution we could stop; from moral confusion and spiritual hollowness that drugs and drink and sex and possessions cannot fix but that more love and better adult moral example, attention, and service can?

Wouldn't you like to believe that we and our leaders would make sure that our personal and collective actions and decisions made it easier rather than harder for children to grow up healthy, safe, and educated, and that our personal, social, business, and public policies and practices made it easier rather than harder for parents to support their families and meet their children's needs? Wouldn't you like to believe that a people who committed to and succeeded in sending the first human to the moon, created an atomic bomb in 41 months during World War II, and led the world in health and information technology could and would tackle and solve their children's problems with the same *can-do* verve and will?

Wouldn't you like to believe that enough Americans would heed God's warning, issued by King David, that "He shall save the children of the needy, and shall break in pieces the oppressor"? How can those of us who call ourselves Christians and worship a poor child born in a manger to a carpenter and a righteous woman named Mary not stand up and fight for all children?

Well, I believe we can help our children believe again in America by taking a Stand for them on June 1, 1997, in local communities just as we did on June 1, 1996, at the Lincoln Memorial. For the choices we make and stands we take now for our children's and nation's futures, whose trajectories of success and failure are inextricably intertwined, will shape America's fate in the new era.

The State of America's Union

I can see a world where children do not learn hatred in their homes. I can see a world where mothers and fathers have the last and most important word.

I can see a world in which one respects the rights of one's neighbors. I can see a world in which all adults protect the innocence of children.

I can see a world in which people do not call each other names based on skin color. I can see a world free of acts of violence. I can see a world in which people of all races and all religions work together to improve the quality of life for everyone.

I can see this world because it exists today in small pockets of this country and in a small pocket of every person's heart. If we will look to God and work together—not only here but everywhere—then others will see this world too and help to make it a reality.

Mrs. Rosa Parks in *Quiet Strength*

If I could sit down for justice, you can stand up for children.

Mrs. Rosa Parks, Stand For Children
1997 Honorary Co-Chair

In his 1997 State of the Union address, nearly upstaged by the media's and America's obsession with O.J. Simpson, President Clinton announced, "The state of our Union is strong."

But is it? By what measures? Aren't the fissures from deep racial, economic, family, and spiritual fault lines everywhere threatening to crumble America's house?

How strong is our Union when U.S. children under 15 are suffering from a firearm death rate 12 times higher than the *combined rates* of 25 other industrialized countries, according to the Centers for Disease Control and Prevention? How strong is the union between parents and children when 3.1 million children are reported neglected and abused every year? How strong is the union between mothers and fathers when one in three children is born out of wedlock, divorce deprives almost a million children of a parent every year, child support payments by fathers are 16 times more likely to lag behind than are car

Portrait of Inequality:
White, Black, and Hispanic Children

78 percent of White children live with both parents,
    but 39 percent of Black children
    and 67 percent of Hispanic children do.

63 percent of White children live in homes their parents own,
    but 28 percent of Black children
    and 33 percent of Hispanic children do.

23 percent of White children and over 27 percent of Hispanic children have both a
    father at work and a mother at home,
    but 8 percent of Black children do.

30 percent of White children have a parent who completed college,
    but 13 percent of Black children
    and 8 percent of Hispanic children do.

71 percent of White children are covered by private health insurance,
    but 44 percent of Black children
    and 38 percent of Hispanic children are.

16 percent of White children are poor,
    but over 41 percent of Black children
    and over 39 percent of Hispanic children are.

19 percent of White children live in central cities,
    but over 48 percent of Black children
    and 40 percent of Hispanic children do.

7 of every 1,000 White and Hispanic infants die in the first year of life,
    but 16 of every 1,000 Black infants do.

6 percent of White and Hispanic infants are born at low birthweight,
    but 13 percent of Black infants are.

payments, and domestic violence stalks spouses in every race and income group as the Simpson case shows?

How strong is the union between Blacks and Whites and men and women when affirmative action backlash stalls the slow progress of the last 30 years in breaking the centuries-old affirmative action for White men? Blacks and women make up a small minority in corporate and legal corridors of power. Women make up only 11 percent of congressional power and Blacks only 7 percent, although they make up 51 and 13 percent of the population respectively.

How strong is our economic union when the gap in income between the rich and the middle class and poor is at its widest level in decades? The

How America Stands

Among industrialized countries, the United States ranks:

1st	in military technology
1st	in military exports
1st	in Gross Domestic Product
1st	in the number of millionaires and billionaires
1st	in health technology
1st	in defense expenditures
18th	in the gap between rich and poor children
16th	in living standards among our poorest one-fifth of children

17th	in efforts to lift children out of poverty
18th	in infant mortality
17th	in low-birthweight rates
Below average	in math scores among 41 countries
Last	in protecting our children against gun violence

According to the Centers for Disease Control and Prevention, our country's firearm death rates of children under 15 are far higher than the *combined rates* of 25 other industrialized countries:

U.S. firearm death rate for children under 15:	**12** times higher
U.S. firearm homicide rate for children under 15:	**16** times higher
U.S. firearm suicide rate for children under 15:	**11** times higher
U.S. firearm accident rate for children under 15:	**9** times higher

Three of every four children murdered in the 26 countries combined were American children. Five of the countries had no firearm deaths of children, and five had no firearm suicides or murders.

top 5 percent of families got a 46 percent increase in real, inflation-adjusted income since 1979, while the poorest fifth of families lost 9 percent. The 1995 salary increases received by 35 CEOs of large companies could have lifted 17,000 children out of poverty.

How strong is our civic union when only 49 percent of registered voters go to the polls—the lowest proportion since before the Great Depression?

How strong is our political union when campaign finance practices enable the rich to gain access to political decision makers that children, the poor, the disabled, the elderly, and hard-working families often lack?

How strong is the sense of fairness in our union when, in the 1996 election year, our leaders voted to end "welfare as we know it" by dismantling the 60-year-old safety net and cutting $54 billion over six years in federal assistance from children, families, and legal immigrants without asking a dime of sacrifice from the Pentagon, corporate welfare recipients, or other well-to-do Americans? In fact, Congress gave the Pentagon $11.5 billion it did not need or ask for. Their actions threaten to push another million children into poverty and millions more already-poor children deeper into poverty.

If the measure of our success is love of God and neighbor, spiritual rather than economic growth, truth-telling rather than truth-shaving, service to others over greed and materialism, nonviolence over violence, and family and community bonds over political bonds, then the state of our union is at risk and needs healing. Let us begin the healing process right now with our children. Edmond MacDonald wrote in *Presbyterian Outlook*:

> When God wants an important thing done in this world or a wrong righted, He goes about it in a very singular way. He doesn't release thunderbolts or stir up earthquakes. God simply has a tiny baby born, perhaps of a very humble home, perhaps of a very humble mother. And God puts the idea or purpose into the mother's heart. And she puts it in the baby's mind, and then—God waits. The great events of the world are not battles and elections and earthquakes and thunderbolts. The great events are babies, for each child comes with the message that God is not yet discouraged with humanity, but is still expecting good-will to become incarnate in each human life.

Standing Together for Children We *Can* Make a Difference

On January 20, 1997, 1,440 days from the beginning of the twenty-first century and 47 months from the beginning of the third millennium, an extraordinarily important symbolic convergence occurred, as we celebrated Dr. Martin Luther King Jr.'s birthday and inaugurated the last President of the twentieth century. The key question is whether we are going to just celebrate or truly follow Dr. King.

Many citizens say, "I am not Dr. King and can do nothing to stop child neglect and ill health." But we all have some of Dr. King inside of us, just as we are God's hands and heart and feet and voice in the world. "When evil men plot, good men must plan. When evil men burn and bomb, good men must build and bind. When evil men shout ugly words of hatred, good men must commit themselves to the glories of love. Where evil men would seek to perpetuate an unjust status quo, good men must seek to bring into being a real order of justice," Dr. King counseled.

Some stand mute when children and the poor are treated unjustly because they are afraid of controversy or failure. Dr. King, too, was often afraid—of police dogs, of violence among his followers and foes alike, of disunity in the movement, and of failure in the face of seemingly intractable obstacles. But as a college student I heard him say to take the first step in faith even when the whole stairway is not revealed, and to leave the results to God. He also said, "If you can't run, walk. If you can't walk, crawl, but keep moving." The important thing is to *keep moving*!

Some people stand on the sidelines, saying, "I am not a leader." Yes you are, if you'll let God use you like Shiphrah and Puah. Dr. King was not America's image of a leader any more than seamstress Rosa Parks. He was a Black man in a nation that legalized White supremacy; a preacher and doer of the gospel of service and love in a culture that idolizes material things and power; and a man of nonviolence in a nation that glorifies military might. Great moral movements and leaders are built one committed citizen at a time like Mrs. Parks, who said:

> *I did not get on the bus to get arrested; I got on the bus to go home. Getting arrested was one of the worst days in my life. It was not a happy experience. Since I have always been a strong believer in God, I knew that He was with me, and only He could get me through the next step. I had no idea that history was being made. I was just tired of giving in. Somehow, I felt that what I did was right by standing up to that bus driver.*

"I can't make a difference," countless people say. Oh, yes you can. Parents, communities, youth-serving groups, youths, religious congregations, and businesses are making a real difference, often with the help of private foundations, much-maligned but imaginative and dedicated public officials, and well-targeted federal, state, and local initiatives. Child advocates made a difference in 1995 and 1996 in helping to save Medicaid and school lunches and protections for disabled, neglected, and abused children. We made a difference in helping to get billions of dollars more (rather than cuts) in child care and hundreds of millions more dollars in Head Start. And we made a difference on June 1, 1996, when over 250,000 people of every race, income, faith, age, and state gathered at the Lincoln Memorial to Stand For Children in the largest and most uplifting demonstration of commitment to children in American history. Thousands more stood in 133 local rallies across America. Since June 1, over 150 Children's Action Teams (CATs) in 38 states have continued to Stand For Children in their communities in a variety of ways.

Standing Strong for Healthy Children in Local Communities and on the Internet in 1997

I invite you to join Mrs. Rosa Parks, Rosie O'Donnell, me, and many, many thousands of others to Stand For Children on June 1, 1997, in local communities all across America and in a Virtual Stand For Children Day on the Internet. This year we will focus on *healthy children*—ensuring every child a Healthy Start, the health coverage they need to grow and thrive and reach productive adulthood, and healthy communities that allow them to breathe and walk safely to and learn in school, unimpaired by fear of violence or by untreated health problems.

Why are we standing for healthy children in 1997?

✦ We are standing for healthy children in 1997 because it is unconscionable that *every day* in America children are dying from diseases we

could prevent; are being born too small to live and thrive because their mothers lacked prenatal care; are failing in school because of untreated vision and hearing and learning problems; are being hospitalized with life-threatening asthma and other illnesses that could have been alleviated if their parents could afford needed medication and doctor visits; and are losing private health coverage at a rate of 3,300 a day.

✦ We are standing for healthy children in 1997 because each child is growing up *right now* and needs health protection *right now*, regardless of the state or the parents they chanced to draw. Why should a child's life chances depend on geography? Why should a Massachusetts child have health care that is denied a

Mississippi child whose state chooses not to provide it? Why is a 66-year-old guaranteed health care but a 6- or 16-year-old is not? What makes one child's life more valuable than another's?

✦ We are standing for healthy children in 1997 because healthy children learn better. Imagine sitting all day or week in school with a toothache because your parents can't afford to take you to a dentist. Imagine spending days in a hospital recovering from measles when a cost-effective immunization could have prevented it. Imagine never being able to run and play and dance and romp because your untreated strep throat led to rheumatic fever that damaged your heart. Imagine not being able to listen to music or your family's conversation or the whispered jokes of playmates because your parents couldn't afford medical care and you lost your hearing after your ear infection didn't get treated. Imagine your frustration at being unable to see the blackboard because you don't have glasses.

✦ We are standing for healthy children in 1997 because nearly 10 million children are uninsured in America and the number is growing every day. Nine out of 10 uninsured children live in families that work; seven out of 10 are White; six out of 10 live in two-parent families. If your family is very poor, or on welfare, you can get Medicaid. If you are well-to-do and don't have to work, you can afford to buy health insurance for your children. If you are a parent in the middle—earning somewhere between $15,000 and $50,000 a year—and your employer does not provide health coverage for your family, you often cannot protect your children's health. This could happen to your child or grandchild or mine in this economic climate. If our leaders take only small and piecemeal steps and cover only half of uninsured children and private coverage continues to erode, by the year 2000 there still will be 7.6 million uninsured children. Which of them or us would want our children uninsured? Surely we can do better than this.

✦ We are standing for healthy children in 1997 because it is disgraceful that the world's leader in health technology ranks eighteenth in the industrialized world in infant mortality rates and last in low-birthweight rates. If America's children faced the same infant mortality rate as Japanese children, over 15,000 more U.S. babies would have survived in 1994.

✦ We are standing for healthy children in 1997 because taxpayers benefit when children are healthy. MinnesotaCare is saving taxpayers $2.1 million a month in welfare costs by providing health coverage to its citizens, including over 50,000 children. Every dollar we invest in vaccinating our preschool children saves $3.40 to $16.34 in direct medical costs. Yet one in four preschool children still is not vaccinated although much progress has been made in the past several years. Nine months of prenatal care cost $1,100; one *day* of neonatal intensive care for a low-birthweight baby costs $1,000.

✦ We are standing for healthy children in 1997 because lack of health insurance is a problem we can solve right now and make a huge difference in many child lives. The issue is whether we care enough to build the political will to do it. As one mother, I think it is time to stand up to the men in power and say, "Do it right and do it right now!" Put children's lives and health before capital gains cuts and more unnecessary weapons systems. Healthy, educated children are the most powerful economic growth stimulus and the best defense America can have.

✦ We are standing for healthy children in 1997 because each and every one of us can contribute. Pregnant women can make sure they get prenatal care and do not smoke or drink alcohol. All parents can make sure they do not take drugs or engage in any action that places their children's health at risk. Parents and community outreach campaigns can make sure children are immunized on time. Corporate leaders can stop cutting health care benefits and shifting the burden of health coverage to their employees who cannot afford it or onto taxpayers. Communities can conduct immunization campaigns and make sure clinics are open after 5 p.m. and on Saturdays so working families can get their children vaccinations and check-ups without losing a day of work. States can follow the lead of Minnesota and Massachusetts and dramatically expand state programs to cover uninsured children. All citizens can call and write their representatives and sign and circulate petitions in their congregations, clubs, or places of work during lunch urging state and federal officials to vote for sound health coverage for all children.

✦ We are standing for healthy children in 1997 because it is likely that the 105th Congress will pass some kind of child health bill. It might be a piecemeal bill that leaves millions of children behind, a harmful bill that cuts Medicaid benefits and takes from one group of poor children who need health care to help another group of poor children who are ineligible for Medicaid; or it could be a sound child health bill that covers all 10 million uninsured children and pregnant women and that enables parents to afford and contribute according to their means to timely coverage and the comprehensive services their children need. We must stand up and make sure the latter occurs. Otherwise our leaders may declare that they have taken care of child health while leaving millions of families and children out in the cold.

✦ We are standing for healthy children in 1997 because it is the right and just thing to do! Our Judeo-Christian tradition requires it. "Is there no balm in Gilead? Is there no physician there? Why has the health of my poor people not been restored?" Jeremiah asked. How do we answer him?

CDF does not seek to impose our healthy children agenda on you. If children in your community have a greater need than health care and you want to stand together to address it on June 1, do so and let us know what you do. The important part is pushing children to the top of family, community, congregational, and political consciousness and action agendas, and turning political campaign promises and rhetoric into personal, community, and political action for children. The bottom line is that our nation's priorities are way out of whack.

25 Tips for Standing Effectively for Children

1. **Don't be blinded or bamboozled by political, media, and cultural chaff.** Keep planting your seeds of hope and honesty and hard work and service and leave the harvesting to God.

2. **Ignore labels and just do what you've got to do.** It doesn't matter whether someone calls you liberal, conservative, radical, extreme, or center. Labels don't matter when 2-year-olds are being killed by guns and are dying from lack of health care we could provide.

3. **Talk less and act more.** Peter Marshall, the distinguished preacher, said, "Small deeds done are better than great deeds planned."

4. **Act now with urgency while planning ahead.** Noah did not wait for the flood to come to begin building his Ark. The budget decisions our leaders make this year and next will determine the course of America and the fate of our children today, tomorrow, and in the next century. Many children won't live to see the future if they aren't provided a Healthy and Safe Start right now.

5. **Do something personally to help at least one child or family besides your own.** Anne Frank said, "How lovely to think that no one need wait a moment: We can start now, start slowly changing the world! How lovely that everyone, great and small, can make a contribution toward introducing justice straightaway!"

6. **Don't worry about credit, turf, or critics. Keep doing your work.** Indira Gandhi said her grandfather told her that there are "two kinds of people: those who do the work and those who take the credit. He told me to try to be in the first group; there was less competition there." It doesn't matter who gets the credit, as long as our children get the health care and child care and family supports they need.

What Does America Value?

Our nation *can* afford the investments that children need for a Healthy, Fair, and Safe Start in life—even while we reduce the federal deficit rapidly. Doing so is a matter of making choices, sometimes hard choices that require us and our leaders to exercise the political will to do what is right and reasonable for children. Some of the choices are easier: We can give our children what they need *and* improve the public health *and* cut the deficit:

◆ We can invest $8 billion a year—about 8 cents per American per day—to provide health coverage for each of America's 10 million uninsured children

and

Pay for it *and* improve public health by increasing the cigarette tax to $1 a pack, raising more than $10 billion a year and reducing smoking, especially among young people.

◆ We can add the $8 billion needed to give all eligible children a Head Start, and invest the $6 billion in added funds needed to assure low-income working families the help they need in paying for child care and assuring their children good-quality care

and

Pay for it by ending $4.4 billion a year in tax avoidance by U.S. corporations that claim credit for paying foreign taxes they don't actually pay, and that get tax breaks for foreign subsidiaries that don't actually exist; and by taking out of the defense budget the $11.5 billion that the President has identified as not merely unnecessary but as getting in the way of programs more vital to our national defense.

◆ We can lift millions of children out of poverty by investing $30 billion in job creation, job placement, and training for 3 million low-income parents and in wage subsidies for working families living in poverty

and

We can pay for it by forgoing the huge tax cuts congressional leaders propose to give, which would cost far more than $30 billion and go overwhelmingly to the most well-to-do Americans who need the least help.

◆ Finally, we must invest the $2 billion we need to spend to help communities provide children with safe and positive after-school and summer activities, and to protect children from family violence

and

We can more than pay for these prevention programs to keep children safe by using the money Congress put in a trust fund for that purpose in 1994 but now refuses to direct toward prevention, and by canceling the $500 million in special tax breaks for alcohol fuels (ethanol) and $1.4 billion for drilling and mining uranium, sand, gold, oil, gas, and coal.

7. **Have holding power.** Hang in and hang onto your values and faith in every kind of political weather. Millions of children will continue to perish rather than flourish if sunshine advocates give up when inevitable stormy political weather and low tides come. Persist and insist that children's needs be met.

8. **Stand up and fight the real opponents of children, the poor, and hard-working Americans, rather than each other.** Our children have so many needs and there is *so* much to do. It will take every effort of everyone within and without the child advocacy community to meet them. We must work with each other and reach out to others in every party, race, income, faith, and age group to form powerful coalitions that marry self-interest and altruism without compromising our mission.

9. **Stand together.** Watch out for political divide-and-conquer games. At the wonderful Monterey, Calif., aquarium, I watched little sardines swim together in unified formation. This protects tiny fish from sharks and other predator fish who gulp them up one by one when they stray off alone. If child advocates don't swim together and focus on a few achievable objectives for our children each year, crucial individual child investments will be eaten up one by one. Don't let our leaders pit hungry children against homeless children, children with disabilities against abused children, and mothers who need child care to get off welfare against those already working who need child care to stay off welfare. And don't allow political leaders to squeeze children, the poor, the disabled, working Americans, and legal immigrants into a tiny, segregated budget-cutting box while powerful special interests are exempt.

10. **Learn how to communicate simply.** A Chinese proverb reminds, "Tell me, I'll forget. Show me, I may remember. But involve me, and I'll understand." That's why CDF's Child Watch Visitation program takes community, media, and political leaders out to see and experience first-hand the needs of children, the solutions to those needs, and how everyone can help. As welfare repeal unfolds, bringing in its wake hunger, neglect, and more poverty, put a child, family, and program behind the statistics. During the June 1 Stand For Children Day, when your members of Congress are home, take every single one of them on a Child Watch visit to talk to parents, children, and providers and see the human faces behind the statistics. Take them to a neonatal intensive care unit and let them see the child, parent, and taxpayer costs of low birthweight. I hope Child Watches on child health needs and solutions will go on all over America until our corporate, state, local, and federal leaders feel compelled to act. Ask them what they plan to do to assure jobs, child care, and health care for families.

11. **Don't waste time reinventing the wheel, in endless meetings, or duplicating efforts when there is so much new ground and so many unmet child needs.** CDF does not take positions on or try to work on many of the important children's issues that are addressed effectively by others. All of us must keep seeding, watering, fertilizing, and growing a movement to Leave No Child Behind, which will take many, many planters and tenders.

12. **Reach out to others. Know how and when to collaborate but do not be afraid to lead.** It is always a few people who get done the things that others can follow, adapt, and expand as desired. Margaret Mead said, "Never doubt that a small group of thoughtful, committed citizens can change the world! Indeed, it's the only thing that ever has." Take care to have enough process but not so much that the world moves on and ripe opportunities to help children are lost. It is a hard but necessary struggle to strike the proper balance between leading, collaborating, following, and seizing targets of opportunity.

13. **Don't take *but* for an answer.** How many times have you heard, "I am for (indeed, who can possibly be against?) children— *but* this is unrealistic in light of budget constraints; *but* it will take a lot more time to get done; *but* I don't like this particular proposal or strategy; *but* this is not the right time; *but* you need to build the political support for it and come back; *but* the other party will block it. *But. But!* I have been particularly struck with the child health coverage *buts* I've heard: I'm for all children getting health coverage, *but* we ought to cover their parents too (I agree); *but* we need to balance the budget and there is no money to cover parents or all children; *but* I'm against a new government program; *but* we need to lower

our goal or we won't get bipartisan support; *but* you outside groups ought to get your act together; *but* we must figure out whether to do it through Medicaid or health tax credits or vouchers, or at the state level, or through employers.

14. **Answer their *buts* with our *buts*.** *But* just do it because children are dying every day and that's morally wrong and unneccessary. *But* there are many ways to provide health coverage for children, building on many successful private, state, and federal efforts. *But* we will pay for it in the same way Congress would pay for capital gains tax cuts and corporate welfare (see box, page xx, about choices we can make to ensure health coverage). Ensuring healthy children is not a money issue; it is a moral imperative.

15. **Don't give up when you fail the first, second, fifth, or tenth time.** Saving children is a mission, not a job. Transforming movements take decades to build and big wars have many battles—some of which you win, some of which you lose, and some of whose outcomes are undetermined for a long time. In 1996, we lost the income safety net but helped beat back seven other unjust block-grant proposals that would have repealed child and family nutrition, child protection, and Medicaid. So don't be discouraged and *don't quit.*

16. **Turn challenges into opportunities and work on multiple fronts.** Child advocates must move beyond the unjust welfare law and turn it into *real* welfare reform in states and localities with demands for parental jobs, child care, and health care. We must simultaneously hold the President's, Congress', and states' feet to the fire to restore many unjust cuts and provide our children and legal immigrants a safety net in every state, especially when a recession comes.

17. **Focus on a few important priorities.** Insist on a seat at the decision-making table when critical policy and political choices are made to implement welfare "reform" in states. Share knowledge and good state practices, and work across party and ideological lines to minimize the welfare law's most harmful features.

18. **Do your homework and keep learning new skills.** Leadership in the 1990s and twenty-first century requires leaders who understand the connection between program, policy, community empowerment strategies, politics, technology, and media—how to get our message across simply and stay on message until it is heard. Child and family advocates, therefore, must be strategic, well-informed, technology- and media-literate, and skillfully insistent and persistent in carrying the urgent message about our children's needs and the spiritual, human, and fiscal costs of not meeting them.

19. **Keep weaving a seamless web of community for children and families across constituencies and disciplines.** We need to preach and practice parental responsibility, personal responsibility, community responsibility, corporate responsibility, and political responsibility. Do not accept either/ors about whose responsibility it is to protect children. All of us must. Parents are the first line of defense, but all parents need safe and healthy communities, employers who help them balance work and family obligations, and government that is fair to all children.

20. **Vote.** It should not be so hard to get our leaders and citizens in our wealthy democratic nation to meet every child's needs to be healthy, educated, safe, and protected by nurturing families and caring communities, as every other industrialized nation does. Why is it so hard? Because children do not vote, lobby, or make campaign contributions. Because political leaders respond to those who can affect their bottom lines—reelection. There are no friends in politics without strong constituencies that hold them accountable. Women, particularly, must translate our concerns for children and families into policy and political accountability.

21. **Run for office.** We need more women and child advocates to run for political office and change the priorities too many men still ignore because they do not bear the brunt of caring for children.

22. **Don't let politicians or the media scapegoat children, poor women, and working families for our budget crisis and other national ills.** Are children and poor families responsible for the growing economic inequality and underlying structural problems in our economy, including declining wages, the loss of manufacturing jobs, export of jobs abroad, and the replacement of human work-

ers by technology? Are children responsible for the 220 million guns in circulation that take over 5,500 young lives each year? Can children and poor women control the decisions of corporate and government power-brokers who determine who gets what? Child advocates must make sure that proposals to balance the budget do not do so on the backs of our children and the poor while the powerful and affluent continue to go untouched or get more. If the rich would just get richer a little less quickly, we could afford to meet all our children's needs tomorrow.

23. **Do not be content with the status quo for children. Have a positive agenda.** Don't defend what doesn't work, but do defend and fight for what does—like Head Start and immunizations and child and family nutrition and quality child care, and jobs, jobs, jobs.

24. **Have faith, keep struggling, and remember that God has the final word**—not the President, Congress, governors, celebrities, the media, or corporations. Slave woman Harriet Tubman's faith helped her run an underground railroad of slaves to freedom without losing a single passenger—a record no train line or airline can beat. "'Twa'n't me, 'twas the Lord," Harriet Tubman said. "I always told Him, I trust You. I don't know where to go and what to do, but I expect You to lead me. And He always did." And He always will!

25. **Pray for children, ourselves, and our nation, that we will do what is right by our children.** "Prayer," Gandhi reminded, "is the key of the morning and the bolt of the evening." With prayer we will continue and succeed in building our movement until no child is left behind.

Oh God we pray for food for the famished
Hope for the hopeless
Comfort for the sad
Protection for the helpless
Strength for the sick and stressed
Courage for those committed to children
Justice for the poor as well as the privileged
Peace for those afflicted by war
We ask to do Your will in Your way this day and for as long as we shall live.

Marian Wright Edelman

The New Welfare Law: The Impact on Children and Families

The welfare law that Congress passed and President Clinton signed in the summer of 1996 combines into one statute several radical measures of different types, each one endangering families and children in a different way.

One part ends the six-decades-old guarantee of cash assistance and creates in its place a new block grant with no assurances of help for poor children. The most sweeping measure in the law is this replacement of Aid to Families with Dependent Children (AFDC) with a new program called Temporary Assistance for Needy Families (TANF). The most basic of its changes are:

✦ The AFDC law said states had to give help to all needy families with children (using the state's definition of need). TANF drops this guarantee.

✦ States must require parents to work within two years of receiving cash assistance through TANF, and can shorten that time limit.

✦ States must impose a five-year lifetime limit on TANF aid, and can make the lifetime limit shorter.

✦ TANF gives states a huge amount of discretion in how to use their block grant dollars. Almost all national standards are gone.

A state must file a written plan telling the federal government how it intends to run the TANF program. State decisions are critical: What is the lifetime limit? What kind of work will be required, and when? Which families will be exempt, either from work or from time limits? How much assistance will be provided, to whom, and through what type of agency? Will help be in the form of cash or through other means? What child care will be available, and of what quality? The choices states make will determine whether children are adequately fed, clothed, housed, and cared for and their parents are prepared adequately for work, or families are cast into destitution without skills or hope.

A second, quite different part of the law makes very large budget cuts in America's nutrition safety net and other assistance programs. In these instances, Congress backed away from proposals to end entitlements, block-grant the programs, or otherwise alter their fundamental structure. But Congress did cut these programs by $54.5 billion over six years. Despite talk of enacting very broad budget cuts affecting all Americans to help balance the budget, Congress focused almost all the budget pain on low-income persons, and did most of the damage through the welfare law. Cuts included more than $27 billion over six years from the food stamp program, $7 billion from the children's portion of the Supplemental Security Income (SSI) program, and billions more from the Child and Adult Care Food Program, the Summer Food Service Program for children, the Title XX Social Services Block Grant, and Medicaid.

The third radical change made by the welfare law is its denial of a broad range of public benefits to legal immigrants. While the rules vary from program to program (and, to an extent, from state to state), most legal immigrants already in the country and most of those yet to enter the United States are cut off from eligibility for federal programs (such as SSI and food stamps) and state-run programs (including TANF and Medicaid). The impact will be devastating: Hundreds of thousands of needy legal immigrants will lose life-sustaining nutrition, health, and income maintenance benefits. Those hurt will range from the infants thrown out of child care centers to the seniors thrown out of nursing homes.

Aside from these three broad categories of harm, the law made other changes, some good and some bad. Strengthened child support enforcement, for example, will increase the chance that children will receive support from both parents.

But the overall impact of the new law will be devastating. According to the Urban Institute, more than 1.1 million children will be thrust into poverty, and the poverty of millions who are already poor will be deepened—even assuming that about two-thirds of the parents find work (see Family Income chapter).

If the grimness of this scenario is to be ameliorated at all, it will be because states base their TANF plans on what families and children really need—not on what appears to save the most money, or on myths about families on welfare. Families on welfare, of course, are not all the same, and sensible policies must grow out of an understanding of these differences. Families with preschool children have child care needs different from those of families with children in school; mothers who have not completed high school will compete less effectively for jobs than those with post-high school training. Families living in areas with sparse public transportation may need cars more than they need training programs. State welfare plans that do not take these differences into account may well squander resources and hurt families.

But states also need to remember that the problems many families faced in the past in getting and keeping jobs that could take them off AFDC and pull them out of poverty have not changed just because the name and structure of the program have changed:

✦ In 1994, 46 percent of mothers receiving AFDC had children age 5 or younger living with them.
✦ About half of mothers receiving AFDC in 1994 did not have high school diplomas.

✦ In 1994, 40 percent of all full-time working single mothers with children earned wages below poverty. Incomes are even lower for the many single mothers not working full-time or year-round.
✦ A 1996 study by the Better Homes Fund and the University of Massachusetts Medical Center showed that more than 80 percent of poor mothers had been victims of domestic violence at some point in their lives.

If states do the minimum the law requires, families could lose assistance very rapidly, without any improved prospects for the parents to find and keep employment. But if states provide more than the restrictive approach in the federal law, and give parents the training, child care, and transportation help they may need, families will have a much better chance of escaping poverty and their children's well-being will be better protected.

How the New Federal Cash Assistance Law Works

Assistance to families with children: TANF does not guarantee help to families meeting state rules. Under the old AFDC law, if a family qualified according to state and federal rules, the family had an "entitlement" to help—the state could not turn the family away or put it on a waiting list, even if more families than expected were in need of help. In turn, the state could count on getting added matching funds from the federal government to help meet the extra need.

Under the new TANF law, no family or child, no matter how needy, is guaranteed aid. There are far fewer federal rules, and states have much, much more latitude to set their own rules for eligibility. But even families that meet those rules cannot be assured they will receive aid. If the federal and state funds for the TANF programs seem to be falling short, states are free to turn families away, put people on waiting lists, reduce assistance across-the-board, or change the rules to restrict eligibility further. States are also free to spend more of their own money and to use their own dollars to continue aid for everyone who qualifies. But the federal share of aid remains fixed (except for a special, small, recession-related fund) and the states must pay 100 percent of any additional expenses they choose to incur.

The federal TANF block grant funding combines federal funds that previously were used for cash aid to needy families with children, for work and training programs, and for a variety of services to meet such emergencies as homelessness. While most states probably will continue to provide cash benefits to families out of the block grant, they are no longer even required to use the money in this way. A state could decide to provide only services, such as child care, work programs, transportation, or counseling; or in-kind help, such as vouchers for rent. States can contract with profit-making entities, local governments, nonprofit social service agencies, or religious institutions to determine TANF eligibility, to provide services, and to send out assistance payments. The program rules and the administrative arrangements made do not have to be uniform throughout the state.

On the other hand, if a state is willing to do more than the minimum that the federal law requires, it can give parents effective preparation for work, assure quality child care when parents enter training or employment, and protect children from want.

TANF funding: The federal payment to each state for cash assistance and work programs will remain fixed at the same level (totaling $16.4 billion nationally) each year for the next six years, whether or not downturns in the economy lead to more poverty among families. To receive all of its share from the federal government, a state must spend only *three-quarters* of what it spent as matching funds in 1994. In other words, states are allowed to cut, without penalty, up to one-quarter of their own 1994 spending.

A state will be allocated federal funds based on its spending in the highest of several base years. These base years occurred when caseloads and spending were relatively high. Because the number of families on welfare dropped 15 percent from March 1994 to September 1996, most states will receive more in the first years of the block grant than they would have under the old law. Looking solely at the money available for cash aid, most states have no immediate need to cut benefits under the new law.

A recession, with growing numbers of families needing assistance, would end this favorable situation. There is a special federal contingency fund for states with growing caseloads in times of high unemployment. But that fund is allocated billions of dollars less than what would be needed to cover caseload growth driven by a typical recession. Also, by requiring states to spend 100 percent of their base-year funding before they tap this fund, rather than the usual 75 percent, the law forces states to put up more to get the extra

---

Facts About Mothers and Children on Welfare

✦ In 1994, 13.97 million people received AFDC. About two-thirds of them (9.44 million) were children.

✦ More than seven in 10 AFDC families (72.6 percent) in 1994 had either one or two children. Fewer than one in 10 (9.6 percent) had four or more children.

✦ Only about three in five poor children received AFDC.

✦ Among families receiving AFDC, 37.4 percent were White, 36.4 percent were Black, 19.9 percent were Hispanic, 1.3 percent were Native American, and 2.9 percent were Asian American.

✦ Seventy percent of mothers and children left AFDC within one or two years. But more than half of those who left (57.6 percent) returned to AFDC within two years.

help precisely when they have less. Even without a recession, states that try to make up for all other federal cuts (to legal immigrants, food stamp recipients, or children with disabilities, for example) will find themselves quickly running low on funds.

The law includes additional small sums for states with high population growth and low welfare spending per poor person. The new law also allows up to 30 percent of the TANF block grant to be transferred to the Child Care and Development Block Grant and the Title XX Social Services Block Grant. This raises the danger that some states will transfer large amounts away from

the subsistence needs of families. While Title XX funds cannot be used to pay cash assistance, they could be used to pay for vouchers to assist children left destitute after losing TANF cash aid because of time limits or other reasons. On the other hand, states could use the transferred dollars to cover social services programs they previously funded from state, rather than federal, revenues. The Center on Budget and Policy Priorities estimates that the transfer provision, combined with allowing states to reduce their level of welfare spending, will let states withdraw as much as $38 billion from welfare and work programs over the next six years.

Welfare Time Limits

Of the 39 states that had filed state TANF plans* by the end of 1996, five set lifetime limits shorter than the federal limit of five years (60 months):

+ **Florida:** 48 months.
+ **Georgia:** 48 months.
+ **Indiana:** 24 months (extensions possible).
+ **Montana:** 24 months (extensions possible).
+ **Utah:** 36 months (extensions possible).

Three states (Connecticut, Massachusetts, and Washington) have indicated plans to continue paying benefits after five years either with state funds or under a waiver.

A number of states, whether or not their lifetime limits are less than five years, have limited the number of months during which a family can receive welfare in a particular time period:

+ **Arizona:** 24 months out of 60 consecutive months.
+ **California:** (governor has proposed) 12 months followed by 12 consecutive months without assistance.

+ **Connecticut:** 21-month limit (six-month extensions in some cases).
+ **Florida:** 24 months out of 60 consecutive months (36 out of 72 for some cases).
+ **Louisiana:** 24 months out of 60 consecutive months.
+ **Massachusetts:** 24 months out of 60 consecutive months.
+ **Ohio:** 36 months out of 60 consecutive months.
+ **Oregon:** 24 months out of 84 consecutive months.
+ **South Carolina:** 24 months out of 120 consecutive months.
+ **South Dakota:** Six months out of 12 consecutive months for two-parent families.
+ **Tennessee:** 18 consecutive months must be followed by an unspecified period off TANF.
+ **Virginia:** 24 months out of 60 consecutive months.

*These state plans are subject to change.

TANF time limits: States can choose the length of time families with children can receive assistance, but this cannot exceed five years, cumulatively, during the lifetime of the recipient. A family on aid for four years, off for a decade, then on for one year hits its lifetime limit. (Time spent on TANF as a child, however, does not count against the five-year limit a person faces when seeking aid as an adult parent.)

States also can choose to limit the duration of aid for a single spell on welfare. For example, the state might have a lifetime limit of five years, but also say that no person can be on welfare for more than two years in any 10-year period. Of the 39 states that filed plans by the end of 1996, 12 chose periods of less than five years for such consecutive time limits. Eleven of these were 24 months or less; in South Carolina, for example, a family is eligible for no more than two years in a 10-year period.

Under the new law, when a family reaches the time limit, it loses all cash or other TANF aid, although the family can continue to receive assistance under other programs, such as food stamps, subsidized child care, and Medicaid. If a mother works each day, but at wages so low she still qualifies for some cash aid, she still will lose all cash assistance at the end of the time limit.

The law allows a state to exempt up to 20 percent of the caseload from the five-year time limit. But in the past, parents with disabilities and parents caring for dependents with disabilities have made up close to 30 percent of the AFDC caseload, a proportion that exceeds the TANF cap on exemptions even before considering such groups as families living in areas of high unemployment, or elderly grandparents caring for grandchildren. Other problems, such as lack of child care or a child's bout with an illness that is not disabling but makes it difficult for a parent to work enough hours to make ends meet, are unlikely to compete successfully for the limited exemptions from the time limit.

A state can set up a separate program and spend its own money to provide continuing assistance after time limits run out. As of late 1996, several states were considering such plans.

Work requirements: There are two forms of work requirements under TANF. One calls for TANF parents to participate in work activities—defined quite narrowly to exclude most forms of training—within 24 months. States also are allowed to require work sooner. Virginia, for example, has chosen to require work within 90 days. A second work provision in the law requires all able-bodied adults to begin to work for their benefits through some form of community service within two months of receiving aid. States may opt out of this second requirement, which will take effect in August 1997 and will force participating states to arrange community service placements at the same time that they are arranging work activities for other TANF parents. Eight out of 39 states filing state plans as of late 1996 opted out of the community service provision.

The law calls for gradually increasing the proportion of the caseload engaged in work, from 25 percent of single parents in Fiscal Year 1997 to 50 percent in Fiscal Year 2002 and beyond. (If the state's caseload is declining for reasons other than benefit cutoffs, the required participation rate is lower.) For two-parent families, the work requirements are even higher—90 percent of such families must have at least one parent at work in 1999. The states' track record in promoting work among two-parent families, even though they are among the easiest to place, does not inspire confidence. In 1995, under the former JOBS program, more than half of the states failed to engage even 50 percent of the two-parent families in work activities.

The hours a parent must work before being counted as working rise too, from 20 hours per week in Fiscal Year 1997 to 30 hours in Fiscal Year 2002, effectively ruling out part-time jobs that would enable parents to attend school or training. The law allows states to exempt from work requirements parents with children younger than 1. Thirteen states, by the end of 1996, had decided to exempt these families.

Unlike the prior law, the new law excludes most forms of training and education from the kinds of activities that count toward the work requirement. High school equivalency training does not count, unless the parent is younger than 20.

Enrollment in college generally does not count, either, although 20 percent of the caseload may be placed in one-year vocational training courses. Parents also may participate in on-the-job training, job search (for 12 weeks), job readiness activities, or community service work. States may help arrange work by subsidizing wages paid by for-profit or nonprofit employers.

Because half of all parents on welfare have not completed high school, many states, up to now, have made education and training important components of their welfare-to-work programs. Before the new welfare law was adopted, many states had federal waiver approval to run experimental work programs, and they can continue to operate them even if their work definitions conflict with the new law (by including more education and training, for example). But even without the waiver authority, states that wish to continue some education and training can do so by providing the maximum training that does count under federal rules and by providing additional training with state or federal dollars, even when those activities will not count toward the narrow federal work requirement.

Child care: Any plan that is serious about promoting families' transitions from welfare to work must ensure sufficient child care help for as long as a family's earnings are low enough to require such assistance. Adequate help to pay for care and the availability of enough quality care have been problems for welfare families as well as for low-income working families. The latter, in particular, often have languished on long waiting lists for child care assistance.

In the TANF law, Congress failed to give the states the means to provide decent care for all children of families leaving welfare for work, much less for the children from other low-income working families. Congress is requiring unprecedented numbers of recipients to work, but did not provide enough child care funding to make that feasible. Furthermore, the new law offers no guarantee that families with young children will receive help with child care, or that child care will meet minimal standards (see Child Care and Early Education chapter).

Other important changes: The TANF law includes many other very important provisions:

✦ States can choose to cut off or reduce benefits to *children* as well as to the parent, if the parent is found not to have participated in work or not to have cooperated with child support enforcement efforts.

✦ Minor parents can receive TANF funds only if they are living at home or in another adult-supervised setting. A teen mother must attend high school or an alternative educational or training program as soon as her child is 12 weeks old.

✦ States can pay lower benefits to residents moving in from other states (as of late 1996, seven states had chosen to do this).

✦ States must have objective criteria for the delivery of benefits, provide for the fair and equitable treatment of applicants and recipients, and provide opportunities for recipients to appeal decisions. But most of the prior law's protections against arbitrary actions and discriminatory rules are gone.

The TANF law also includes an important Medicaid protection. Even if a family loses cash assistance because of the new time limits or other rules, it still will be eligible for Medicaid benefits. Congress said states must give Medicaid to children and caretaker relatives if they would have been eligible for AFDC—and Medicaid—under the AFDC rules in effect on July 16, 1996. But states can choose to have separate application procedures for TANF and for Medicaid, reducing the likelihood that families will use the special Medicaid eligibility provision (see Health chapter).

Child support: As discussed in the Family Income chapter in greater detail, the new law's child support provisions are generally positive, making enforcement more likely for both welfare and non-welfare families. But the new child support laws have one devastating provision for welfare families. In the past, if child support payments were collected on behalf of a child on welfare, the family received the first $50 per month. In a typical state, $50 a month increased the income of a family on welfare by 13 percent. The new law ends this $50 pass-through.

Child protection: The new law does not change the federal guarantees of foster care and adoption assistance, or of Medicaid for children in foster care or adoptive homes. But there are many troubling child welfare implications in the new law, as discussed in the chapter on Children and Families in Crisis. If destitution drives more children into foster care, or if the time limits and work rules applied to grandparents and other nonparental relatives discourage them from caring for children, a fragile child welfare system could be pushed past the breaking point.

Budget Cuts

Food stamps: More than half of the budget cuts in the welfare law came in the food stamp program—more than $27 billion over six years. Two-thirds of these cuts are directed at low-income families with children, denying, reducing, or terminating basic nutrition assistance to millions. The nearly 7 million families with children receiving food stamps each will lose an average of $435 in benefits in the first full year of the cuts.

Neither the food stamp program nor other key child nutrition programs (school lunches and breakfasts, Summer Food Service Program, WIC, or the Child and Adult Care Food Program) were structurally altered; they were not made into block grants, and their legal guarantees of food to needy children were not ended. But three large and devastating changes in the food stamp program will have harsh impact on families with children. The new law:

✦ Limits cost-of-living adjustments in food stamps, so that inflation continually will erode families' subsistence food budgets.
✦ Limits the allowable deduction for high shelter costs for families with children, so families will get less food stamp help.
✦ Makes most legal immigrants ineligible for food stamps altogether.

These and other changes in food stamps and child nutrition programs are discussed in the Food and Nutrition chapter.

Supplemental Security Income: The new law cuts billions of dollars by restricting the definition of disability for children seeking to qualify for federal SSI payments. SSI provides cash assistance for low-income aged, blind, or disabled persons. In the past, a child could qualify either because his or her disability could be found in an official list of medical conditions, or because a physician conducted an individualized assessment of the child's functioning and found it to be significantly abnormal for the child's age level. Under the new law, if the child's condition is not in the medical listings, the child will not qualify for SSI. Depending on how the Social Security Administration administers the new criteria, it is expected that 250,000 to 315,000 children with disabilities no longer will be eligible for SSI.

Legal Immigrants

The third major change in the welfare law is its sweeping ban on benefits to *legal* immigrants, children and adults alike. Most legal immigrants will be barred from help under the major low-income programs administered by the *federal* government, most notably food stamps (about 300,000 legal immigrant children will lose food stamps) and SSI. This prohibition applies both to immigrants already in the country (although currently eligible aliens may not lose benefits before mid-1997) and to those who enter after the law takes effect. Legal immigrants will be barred until they become U.S. citizens, or have worked for 40 calendar quarters.

The situation is slightly more complex in low-income programs using federal funds but administered by the *states*, most notably TANF and Medicaid. Legal immigrants already in the country when the welfare law passed can be thrown off TANF and Medicaid (except for emergency medical services) at state option. At least five states by the end of 1996 had decided to cut off TANF benefits to legal immigrants. Legal immigrants entering the country after August 1996 must be barred for five years from receiving aid through TANF, child care, and non-emergency Medicaid. After five years in the country, unless a state has extended its ban, legal immigrants can become eligible when they become citizens or have worked 40 calendar quarters, and if their sponsors' incomes do not disqualify them.

Opportunities to Help Children

It is essential, as parents struggle to support their families and protect their children, that the federal government commit to ending child poverty (see Family Income chapter), that Congress and the President adjust some of the worst provisions in the new law, and that states administer the law in a way that helps parents find family-supporting work.

At the federal level, the law should be changed to:

✦ Invest in job creation, preparation, and placement. The new law provides $13 billion less than what is needed to make its work rules real, according to the Congressional Budget Office. Parents trying to leave welfare need jobs, the opportunity to develop job skills, and effective placement programs. Funds are needed to subsidize wages for community service jobs, and to promote placement in private-sector employment. Education and training activities should count more readily toward the work requirement, so parents can compete for decent wages.

✦ Continue needed assistance to low-wage working families. Months in which a parent works at least 20 hours a week should not count against the time limit.

✦ Restore food stamps for needy families and individuals. Food stamps must keep pace with inflation, and must meet the needs of families with very high housing costs.

✦ Protect children from destitution and family break-up. The federal law should require some form of continued aid to children to prevent destitution if TANF benefits are terminated because of time limits or penalties.

✦ Restore SSI for all children with disabilities.

✦ Restore all essential income, nutrition, and health benefits for legal immigrants.

✦ Assure quality child care for children whose parents work or engage in training, and waive the work requirement if no child care is available for a child younger than 11 (as both houses had voted to do before the welfare bill was changed in a conference committee).

States also must use their new discretion to craft programs that help parents find jobs and that protect children from poverty. States must:

✦ Build education and training back into the work program. Even without a change in the federal law, states can continue to provide education and training, although some activities may not count toward the federal minimum-participation rate.

✦ Allow partial assistance to families with low earnings as long as their earnings are below poverty, using state dollars, if necessary, when the time limit has been reached.

✦ Provide child care for all children under 11 when parents are required to work or get training.

✦ Help make transportation to work affordable and accessible.

✦ Exempt from the time limit specific categories of families, such as those in which a parent has a disability or is caring for a dependent with a disability, families in areas of high unemployment, and families in which grandparents or other relatives are caring for children. States should use state funds, when necessary, to pay benefits for these families when the federal cap on exemptions from the five-year limit is exceeded.

✦ Vigorously enforce the new child support rules, and re-establish the $50 pass-through.

✦ Use the option to exempt parents with children younger than 1 from the work requirement. (These parents still could participate voluntarily in work.)

✦ Use partial, not total, cutoffs of aid to families for noncompliance with the law's work and child support provisions, to minimize harm to children.

✦ Choose options to cover legal immigrants.

Family Income

America's ongoing economic recovery has benefited the wealthiest one-fifth of households while others lost income between 1989 and 1995, leaving the gap between rich and poor at historically high levels. While 1995 showed a bigger jump in family income and a bigger drop in child poverty than did most recent years, still our nation had more children in poverty—nearly 15 million—than in any year between 1966 and 1991. The effects of the growth in the economy over the past two decades have been terribly uneven, and tens of millions of American parents continue to find it hard to get stable, family-supporting jobs with wages and benefits that are adequate to keep home and hearth together.

Rather than moving toward providing parents with the supports they need to work and keep their children out of poverty, however, Congress in 1996 did precisely the opposite, by passing a welfare reform law that will cut help to working and non-working families alike, dramatically increase economic insecurity, and further widen the gap between rich and poor. It will make 1.1 million additional children (mostly from working families) poor, and make millions of poor children poorer. The new law purportedly is premised on the idea of putting millions more welfare parents to work, but it fails to address fundamental labor market problems that make it hard for low-wage workers to find jobs that support their families, and it actually cuts federal resources for job training (see Welfare chapter).

The new welfare law not only ended the six-decades-old federal guarantee of cash assistance to poor families with children (meager as the help too often was) and put rigid time limits on that assistance. It also made huge cuts, totaling $54 billion over six years, in disability, anti-hunger, income maintenance, and health programs for lower-income working as well as non-working families with children, while much of the rest of federal spending went untouched. When historians look back on the damage that the welfare law will cause in the years ahead, its passage almost certainly will stand out as the most important event of 1996 for America's families and children.

There was also, however, a range of welcome developments in 1996—a few positive steps and some important, hard-won victories against efforts to slash help for low-income children and families even more deeply than the final welfare law did. Congress rejected efforts to block-grant and turn over to the states food stamps, school lunches and breakfasts (see Food and Nutrition chapter), Supplemental Security Income (SSI) for children with disabilities, and foster care and adoption assistance (see Children and Families in Crisis chapter). Early proposals to take more than $23 billion from working families with children through Earned Income Tax Credit (EITC) cuts were defeated. And the welfare law's huge cuts in other programs were tens of billions of dollars less than what initially was proposed. The law's child support enforcement provisions mostly had bipartisan support and mostly were improvements. Separate from the welfare law, the minimum wage was increased for the first time in five years. And continued growth in the economy led to declines in unemployment and child poverty. Still, American child poverty rates remain inexcusably high—well above adult poverty rates, well above child poverty rates 15 to 30 years ago, and well above child poverty rates in other wealthy nations. Our high child poverty rates threaten the nation's social and economic future.

Gains Elude America's Low- and Middle-Income Families

For many Americans, 1996 brought good news. The economy grew for the fifth consecutive year—in some quarters, fairly robustly. The official unemployment rate fell to 5.4 percent in December 1996. Since May 1974, only one month had a lower unemployment rate than the 5.1 percent rate in August 1996. Corporate profits boomed and the stock market posted huge gains.

But far less of this good news is trickling down to most American families than is healthy for them, the economy, or America's children. Despite some real gains for American households, 1995 still left the bottom four-fifths of American households with incomes significantly below 1989 levels. For example, the poorest one-fifth of households had an average income of $8,473 in 1979, $8,629 in 1989, and $8,350 in 1995, when adjusted for inflation. The real gainers over the past decade and a half have been the wealthiest one-fifth of households. Their average income was 16 times the average income of the poorest fifth of households in 1979, but 23 times as high in 1995. The top 5 percent of households did especially well: Their average incomes rose 43 percent from 1979 to 1995.

These data do much to explain why so many Americans continue to feel economically stressed, insecure about their near-term futures, and worried about their children's long-term prospects, despite ongoing national economic growth and gains in average per capita personal income. The averages disguise the fact that most Americans simply have not been benefiting; the gains during the period have gone almost exclusively to the richest Americans, making U.S. income distribution more and more unequal.

Aside from the layoffs they experience, see their neighbors experience, or learn of on the nightly news, America's working families feel a range of direct effects of a changing economy.

✦ Families with children are falling behind. The median incomes of families with children have not kept up with the growth in the economy, or even with inflation; they fell by 3 percent

✦ In 1995, 14.7 million U.S. children—21 percent—were poor. That's almost twice the adult poverty rate of 11 percent.

✦ The median income of families with children fell 3 percent between 1973 and 1994, while the income of families without children rose 13 percent.

✦ The minimum wage increases to $5.15 an hour in September 1997. Full-time, year-round work at that wage equals only 83 percent of the poverty line for a three-person family.

✦ Fewer than one in five child support cases handled by state agencies in Fiscal Year 1994 had any support paid.

from 1973 to 1994, while the median income of families *without* children rose 13 percent, when adjusted for inflation. Before 1983, families with children had median incomes that were higher than those of families without children, but since then this has reversed. In part, the divide between families with and without children reflects a growing generational divide: Young workers in their child-bearing years are suffering most of the brunt of economic losses. For example, 20- to 29-year-old workers had hourly wages in 1995 (adjusted for inflation) that were only four-fifths of what their parents' generation earned at the same age in 1973.

✦ It takes two earners to support children. Millions of families have been forced to send a second parent into the work force to compensate for the lower wages now earned by one worker. But even though far more families are sending both parents to work than did so 20 or 30 years ago, declining wages per worker mean that total family incomes don't always keep up—especially after deducting families' new child care and other work-related costs. Also dragging down the average incomes of families with children has been the ongoing growth in

the number of single-parent families, whose incomes are much lower than those of two-parent families. A complex mix of causes, cultural and economic (for example, young men with wages below poverty are far less likely to get married than those with wages above poverty), has driven the increases in out-of-wedlock births and in divorces of parents, and has had the effect of reducing the incomes of families in which children live.

✦ Job-related benefits are shrinking. Adding to families' hard times, fewer and fewer employers are providing essential fringe benefits (see Health chapter).

The growth of income inequality got an un-needed boost when Congress and the President enacted the new welfare law. The Urban Institute projects that the law, when fully phased in, will cause one-fifth of America's families with children to lose an average of $1,310 each year in social welfare benefits, even after making optimistic estimates of increased employment for welfare recipients.

Most of these losses will not be because families lose Temporary Assistance for Needy Families (TANF, which replaces Aid to Families with De-

INCOME INEQUALITY

Since 1985, the richest 5 percent of U.S. families have received a larger share of the nation's income than the poorest 40 percent.

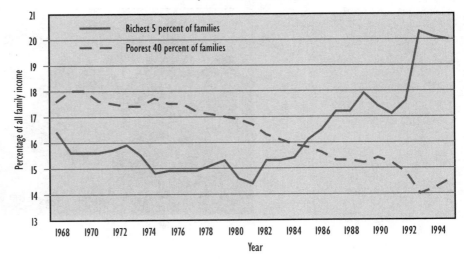

Share of total U.S. family income going to rich and poor families, 1967–1995

Richest 5 percent of families

Poorest 40 percent of families

Percentage of all family income

Year

Source: U.S. Census Bureau.

pendent Children), but because families, including working families, lose food stamps, SSI for disabled children, and other benefits. Exacerbating the damage from losing such supports, many lower-income working families also will suffer losses in earnings because of the new competition for low-wage jobs from the millions of welfare recipients being forced into work—an effect of the law outside the scope of the Urban Institute study.

One modest improvement that 1996 brought was the first minimum-wage increase since 1991, when the wage was lifted to $4.25 per hour. The 1996 law raised the minimum wage to $4.75 in October 1996, and will raise it to $5.15 in September 1997. Even with the 1997 increase, however, the minimum wage for a full-time, year-round job will provide a family of three only 83 percent of what would be needed to keep them out of poverty. Full-time minimum-wage work generally earned between 95 percent and 110 percent of the poverty line for a three-person family from 1961 to 1981, but has been worth less than 85 percent of poverty since 1984. Even while the nation has grown wealthier, Congress has left the minimum wage at these depressed levels, perhaps deferring to business-sector warnings that raising it would prompt job losses; re-

cent studies, however, strongly suggest that this is not true—that moderate minimum-wage increases do not trigger job losses. An inadequate minimum wage does mean, however, more child poverty and more child suffering. In 1995, the share of poor children who lived in households headed by a full-time, year-round worker was at the highest level (21 percent) since these data first were collected in 1975.

Building on the success at the federal level, voters in California and Oregon in 1996 approved ballot initiatives to set their state minimum wages higher than the federal minimum. Two million workers will benefit from California's Proposition 210, which will raise the state minimum wage to $5.75 on March 1, 1998. In Oregon, Measure 36 increased the minimum wage in three stages, raising it to $6.50 in January 1999. Ballot initiatives to raise the minimum wage failed in Montana, Missouri, and Denver, in part because well-funded opponents outspent proponents by wide margins—by 10-to-1 in Missouri, for example.

Another strategy to raise wages has been city-based living-wage campaigns that call for service providers that contract with municipalities to pay wages (about $6.25 to $7.00 an hour, at minimum)

ERODING MINIMUM WAGE

*E*ven after the minimum-wage increase goes into full effect in 1997, minimum-wage earnings from a full-time, year-round job will not come close to lifting a three-person family out of poverty.

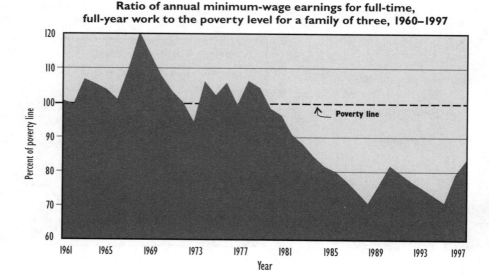

Ratio of annual minimum-wage earnings for full-time, full-year work to the poverty level for a family of three, 1960–1997

Source: U.S. Department of Labor and U.S. Census Bureau. Calculations by Children's Defense Fund. Poverty line is the 1995 level, adjusted for inflation. (CPI-U inflation measure is used.)

sufficient to lift a family out of poverty; most re-quire health benefits as well. Over the past two years, living-wage ordinances have passed in Baltimore, Jersey City, Milwaukee, New York City, and Portland, Ore. Additional campaigns are under way in Boston, Chicago, Los Angeles, Milwaukee County, and Minneapolis–St. Paul.

The congressional majority in 1996 also proposed to help families with children by giving them a $500 per child per year tax credit. (The President proposed a similar credit, phased out for more affluent families and for teenagers.) While there are ways to improve the tax code so struggling families with children receive more help, proposals to give credits that are not "refundable" (available to families with incomes too low to owe income tax) focus all their help where it is least needed: According to the Center on Budget and Policy Priorities, none of a non-refundable $500 tax credit would go to the *28 million* children in the families with the lowest incomes. Virtually all families with annual incomes below $20,000 and many below $30,000 would be excluded. This credit for the three-fifths of families with the most income also would help worsen the budget deficit by tens of billions of dollars, forcing more cuts in programs for the children who need help the most.

Positive Child Support Enforcement Steps

Child support is an urgent public issue, because it affects the fundamental well-being of so many children. In 1994, one in every four children lived in a family with only one parent present in the home. Half of all children spend some of their childhoods in single-parent families.

Losing a parent from the home is often an economic disaster. Half of the 18.7 million children living in single-parent families in 1994 were poor, compared with about one of every 10 children in two-parent families.

Better child support enforcement can produce much more income for children. A 1994 study by the Urban Institute estimated that if child support orders had been established and fully enforced in 1990 for all children with living noncustodial fathers, aggregate child support payments in that year would have been $47.6 billion dollars—nearly three times the child support actually paid, and enough to lift millions of children out of poverty.

Despite the importance of child support enforcement, and dramatic changes in public attitudes and laws, the past decade brought virtually no change in the percentage of mothers with child

---

YOUNG FAMILIES' LOSSES

Between 1973 and 1994, the median income of young families with children dropped by one-third. At the same time, the incomes of older families with children nearly kept pace with inflation, and childless families made modest income gains.

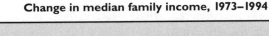

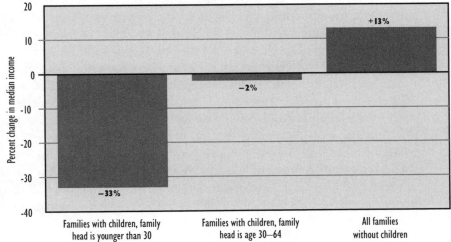

Change in median family income, 1973–1994

Percent change in median income

- Families with children, family head is younger than 30: **−33%**
- Families with children, family head is age 30–64: **−2%**
- All families without children: **+13%**

Source: Tabulations of Census Bureau data by the Center for Labor Market Studies at Northeastern University and Children's Defense Fund. Adjusted for inflation (using CPI-X inflation measure).

Housing and Homelessness

The housing situation of low- and moderate-income Americans has been worsening for a number of years. While incomes of families with children have declined, rent increases have exceeded inflation and much low-income housing has been lost to decay, gentrification, and urban redevelopment.

A generation ago, inexpensive housing units outnumbered the families needing them; today, millions more households need low-cost housing than can find it. The National Low-Income Housing Coalition reported in 1996 that a full-time, minimum-wage income now is inadequate to afford moderate-cost, moderate-quality housing in every one of the 404 metropolitan areas that it studied.

This housing crunch will worsen further because of the new welfare law's cash aid and nutrition cuts. In an early warning of the consequences that may lie ahead for the nation, the Associated Press reported in late 1996 that when Wisconsin implemented its new, stricter welfare policies, hundreds of additional families jammed homeless shelters there.

But even before the new welfare law took effect, the shrinking supply of affordable housing for low-income families was having devastating effects. The U.S. Conference of Mayors reported in 1996 that in the 29 cities it surveyed, families with children made up 38 percent of the homeless population. A study of Philadelphia and New York found *child* homelessness increasing sharply, even while the cities were making progress getting single adults into permanent housing. Nearly one in 10 of New York City's poor children under 5 lived in shelters in 1996. Shelter life breaks up families, disrupts schooling, increases child health problems, and causes children extreme emotional distress.

Middle- and upper-income families that own homes are getting *more* housing help. The cost to the government of their tax breaks—mainly the mortgage interest deduction and the property tax deduction—has increased sharply. More than two-thirds of this tax subsidy goes to families with incomes above $75,000 a year. The deductions do not help families that rent, or that can't afford to buy housing, or whose incomes are too low to use tax deductions.

The federal government, at the same time, is cutting way back on housing assistance for low- and moderate-income families, slashing its support for both public housing and assisted housing like the Section 8 program of rent subsidies for low-income tenants of privately owned housing. Federal housing appropriations have fallen by one-quarter in the past few years. U.S. Department of Housing and Urban Development (HUD) appropriations for Fiscal Year 1996 included *no* new vouchers or certificates for Section 8 housing, and none are being issued in Fiscal Year 1997; in contrast, the number of certificates and vouchers added to increase availability of assisted housing never dropped below 40,000 in any year of the 1980s, and even that level was a drastic reduction from the 1970s. Jason DeParle of the *New York Times* wrote, "The federal government has essentially conceded defeat in its decades-long drive to make housing affordable to low-income Americans."

The U.S. Conference of Mayors found in 1996 that only 28 percent of eligible low-income households in the cities it surveyed

This box was prepared in cooperation with Nancy Bernstine, a staff attorney at the National Housing Law Program, located at 1815 H St. NW, Suite 700, Washington, DC 20006, 202-783-5140.

received housing assistance. Waiting periods for housing in these cities averaged 19 months for public housing and 31 months for Section 8 certificates. Charlotte, N.C., officials expect the lack of new certificates to increase the waiting period for Section 8 help from five years to between 10 and 15 years.

Experts expect the HUD budget squeeze to get even worse over the next few years, because much of the HUD appropriation will have to be used to renew expiring contracts with owners of Section 8 housing. A large number of Section 8 properties constructed by private developers have operated under 20-year rent-subsidy contracts between the owners and HUD. Many of these contracts will expire over the next few years, and the cost of renewing or extending them (to avoid tenants' evictions and landlords' mortgage defaults) will be huge.

Although Congress has failed to provide nearly enough funding for housing, it has *not* fundamentally altered the entire housing program. Proposals in 1995 and 1996 to block-grant federal housing help did not succeed. Neither did Congress pass a proposal to weaken the federal housing law that bans discrimination against families with children by allowing landlords to keep out or evict families with more than two persons per bedroom, regardless of the housing's configuration or bedroom size, or the family make-up. A couple living in a one-bedroom apartment could have lost housing when they had a new baby.

Although these sweeping changes were not made, Fiscal Year 1996 and 1997 appropriations laws and rule changes made by the Clinton Administration were extremely harmful. The preference for local housing authorities targeting housing assistance to the neediest of the poor was suspended; discretion was broadened for local authorities to rent more units to higher-income households that need smaller subsidies (and fewer units

to needier households), and to charge a minimum rent to even the most destitute families; procedures were changed to make it easier for local housing authorities and Section 8 landlords to evict tenants or not to renew leases; the local-market rent measurement that determines maximum Section 8 subsidies was reduced, making less housing available and raising the share paid by families; a 90-day waiting period was imposed, delaying when a local housing authority can reissue to another family a Section 8 certificate or voucher turned in by a family no longer needing it; and the longstanding requirement that a local housing authority must replace every unit of public housing lost through demolition or sale was suspended.

Against this bleak picture, some more optimistic signs did appear in 1996. A study by the Barnard–Columbia Center for Urban Policy endorsed HUD's community-based Continuum of Care process for identifying and responding to the needs of homeless people. And while they cannot compensate for the badly shrunken federal housing presence, thousands of local housing and community development groups are building tens of thousands of new low-income units each year and in some cases helping to reclaim whole neighborhoods. They typically package financing from the Community Development Block Grant, the federal Low Income Housing Tax Credit, and other federal funding streams, and funds from state and local governments, foundations, and private sources, with support from key groups like the Local Initiatives Support Corporation (LISC), the Enterprise Foundation, and the Neighborhood Reinvestment Corporation.

But turning around the crisis of housing affordability will require a renewed commitment by the federal government, as well as much more active involvement of state and local governments, in developing large amounts of low-income housing.

support awards, the average child support payment due, or the average amount received (after adjusting for inflation). Nationally, of the 5.4 million women who were due support (far below the number eligible for such orders), only slightly over half received the full amount due, while a quarter received partial payment and a quarter received nothing at all.

A major contributor to these dismal data has been the poor performance of the federal–state child support enforcement system. That system focuses on serving welfare families and non-welfare families that ask it for help. It has made progress in paternity establishment, but little progress overall. Fewer than one out of every five cases served by state agencies had any child support paid in Fiscal Year 1994—a proportion that has risen only slightly since Fiscal Year 1990. The number of non-welfare families seeking state enforcement help has grown dramatically, so that considerably more families are getting help, but the share of all families that are helped is not growing, and states' performance levels remain unacceptable.

There are ways for states to do better. For example, Massachusetts created a centralized child support system that compensated for staffing shortages by using computers to search multiple databases, including bank and employment records, and to begin collection actions automatically. It adopted a number of cutting-edge paternity and enforcement techniques, such as liens on bank accounts to collect past-due support. In three years, the state was able to collect about 80 percent of all child support due from noncustodial parents living in Massachusetts, and voluntary paternity acknowledgments skyrocketed.

The new welfare law makes a broad array of child support changes that are generally very positive. These changes move states toward more centralized, automated systems that can take steps to locate noncustodial parents and to begin enforcement actions automatically, which may help stretch scarce staff time and resources. The new law also requires all states to have in place certain practices that pioneering states have shown to be effective. For example, it creates both national and state reporting registries for new hires, so that payroll deductions of child support can begin quickly

when a noncustodial parent changes jobs; and it requires states to have the authority to withhold, suspend, or restrict the use of drivers' licenses, professional or occupational licenses, and some recreational licenses, to encourage payment of child support. The new law improves interstate enforcement by bolstering federal services to locate parents across state lines and by requiring all states to have common paternity procedures in interstate cases.

On the other hand, the law ends the rule that previously required states to let a welfare family keep $50 of the child support paid each month on the child's behalf by an absent parent to the state. This $50 "pass-through" let the family reap a little benefit from child support. Since the median state welfare payment is only $389 a month for a mother and two children, this loss will mean real hardship for families and will reduce their incentives to help child support enforcement efforts. However, the new law also changes previous practice and gives children formerly on welfare priority over the state in most instances when back child support is collected and support is owed both to the child and to the state.

Child Poverty Remains High

Declining wages, growing inequality, declining incomes for many families with children, more single-parent families, grossly inadequate public income supports (even before the new welfare law's effects bite deeper), and a too-often-ineffectual child support enforcement system hurt many American families. But our nation's failings toward children's basic economic security are most starkly revealed by America's level of child poverty.

In 1995, the number of children living in families with incomes below the poverty line ($15,569 for a family of four that year) declined for the second year in a row, and 600,000 fewer children were poor in 1995 than in 1994. This was good news, but the first three years of the economic recovery, from 1991 to 1994, had brought virtually no drop in poverty. When improvement finally came in 1995, it was less than half the yearly improvement seen from 1964 to 1969, when a vigorous economy and a vigorous anti-poverty policy reduced poverty at a rate of 1.2 million children per year. In 1995, *14.7 million* children (21 percent of America's children) were living in poverty, 2.1 million more than in 1989.

Very young and minority children bear the worst brunt of this society's very high child poverty rates. One in four children under 6 (24 percent) and more than one in three Hispanic (40 percent) and Black (42 percent) children live in poverty.

Contrary to stereotypes, in two out of three poor families with children, someone worked at least part of the year. In 1995, the proportion of poor families that were headed by someone who worked during the year was higher than at any time since at least 1975. The average poor family with children got more than twice as much income from work as from welfare.

If America's periods of economic recovery do not start pulling children out of poverty sooner, faster, and for more years than they have been, America's child poverty problem never will show lasting improvement. Rather, we will just repeat what has happened in every economic cycle since 1973—the periods of recession push more children into poverty than the growth periods pull out.

As a result of these cycles:

✦ Children have been getting poorer as the nation grows richer. Since 1969, the gross domestic product doubled, but the child poverty rate rose from 14 percent to 21 percent.

✦ By 1995, America's children were nearly twice as likely as adults to be poor (21 percent versus 11 percent).

✦ Children in the United States are 1.6 times more likely to be poor than those in Canada, two times more likely than those in Britain, and three times more likely than those in France or Germany, even though the United States is the wealthiest of these nations and has lower unemployment levels.

Our child poverty rate is the result of a job market and public policies that fail to help poor and moderate-income families become more economically secure. While debates rage around welfare, our public policy shortcomings are much broader: Most wealthy nations use a range of pro-family policies (including paid parental leave, assured child support for children in single-parent families, and children's allowances) to lift millions of children out of poverty. If the United States lifted out of poverty the same proportion of otherwise-poor children as do Britain, France, Belgium, Denmark, Finland, Luxembourg, Norway, and Sweden, our child poverty rate would be under 10 percent rather than over 20 percent. If the United States lifted out of poverty the same proportion of otherwise-poor children as it does otherwise-poor senior citizens, the child poverty rate would be 5.1 percent, and there would be 11 million fewer poor children.

Before the 1996 welfare law, government policy to lift children out of poverty had been improving—too slowly, but improving—for nearly a decade. Expansions of the EITC, improvements in food stamp benefits, the extension of AFDC to more two-parent families, and SSI improvements for children with disabilities were among the positive changes. Taking into account taxes and certain non-cash benefits, these improvements caused the number of children (many from working families) removed from poverty by government benefit programs to double between 1983 and 1995, according to the Center on Budget and Policy Priorities. Now the welfare law has rolled back substantially three of these four improvements (the EITC was left largely intact), and also made numerous other harmful changes.

As a result, the Urban Institute has estimated that the welfare law not only will push 1.1 million more children into poverty, but will push already-poor children deeper into poverty—projecting that more than 4 million already-poor families will lose an average of $1,040 each, per year.

Child poverty exacts a terrible toll from children—and the nation. Poor children are two times more likely than nonpoor children to have stunted growth, iron deficiency, and severe asthma. Health officials in Kansas and Maine report that low-income children are three times more likely to die during childhood. A new government study in 1996 showed that poverty placed children at greater risk of dying before their first birthdays than did a mother's smoking during pregnancy. An earlier U.S. Department of Education study found that every year spent in poverty adds to the chances that a child will fall behind grade level by age 18. The Children's Defense Fund, assisted by a team of noted social scientists, estimated in the 1994 book *Wasting America's Future* that every year of child poverty at current levels will cost the nation at least $36 billion in lost future productivity alone, because poor children will be less educated and less effective workers.

Alternatives to Welfare That *Help* Children and Families

The welfare system has been flawed not just because it discouraged work, but because it left far too many children and families in poverty. The new welfare law seeks to force people to work by cutting off assistance. More work likely will result, but deep and damaging poverty for children is inevitable if no other steps are taken. A look at alternatives employed by two states shows that there are far less harmful ways to encourage parents to work and to enable them to lift their children out of poverty.

New York State's Child Assistance Program (CAP), begun in 1988 and now operating in 14 counties, allows families to combine work with cash assistance in a way that has paid off for participating families *and* for the state.

Families that take part voluntarily in CAP receive a basic benefit that is about one-third less than the AFDC payment level. To participate, a family must have a child support order for at least one child. Unlike AFDC benefits, which typically were reduced by $1 for every $1 earned through work, CAP benefits are reduced by 10 cents per dollar until the family's income reaches the poverty line, and then are reduced by 67 cents per dollar up to one and one-half times the poverty level ($19,470 for a family of three in 1996). A parent who earns at least $350 a month has more income under CAP than under AFDC.

A five-year evaluation of CAP in three counties, completed in 1996 by Abt Associates, shows that the program increases the number of parents who work and somewhat decreases their length of stay on welfare. CAP families raised their average monthly earnings to $679, from $93 in the month

before they participated. Even more promising, according to Abt Associates, families that had the option to participate in CAP were less likely than others to return to welfare after leaving.

CAP saved federal, state, and local governments $50 million over five years because of reduced use of AFDC, food stamps, and Medicaid, and increased child support collections. CAP's return was better than 10-to-1: It cost $237 more per household to administer than AFDC, but savings amounted to $2,603 per household.

The Minnesota Family Investment Program (MFIP) takes another approach to encouraging work. Families in seven Minnesota counties receive a single payment combining the value of AFDC and food stamps. MFIP families with earnings from work start with a 20 percent bonus in their basic assistance. The benefit then is reduced as earnings increase, but less precipitously than AFDC's dollar-for-dollar penalty. MFIP families also are eligible for child care assistance—key to enabling them to find and keep jobs.

An 18-month evaluation by the Manpower Demonstration Research Corp. (MDRC) found that MFIP had positive results even for the families generally thought to be hardest to serve. MFIP increased work and decreased poverty for urban recipients who had received welfare benefits for at least two years (half of those studied had been on welfare for five years or longer). Seventy-six percent of MFIP participants found employment at some point during the 18 months studied, compared with 59 percent of a control group of regular AFDC recipients. MFIP participants earned more than the control group and, because earnings were combined with the MFIP income supplement, these long-term recipients also were more likely to get out of poverty. Sixty-six percent of the MFIP participants, in fact, had incomes above poverty. MFIP's employment gains and poverty reductions are as significant as or better than any similar U.S. programs studied thus far.

Another Minnesota initiative has played a significant role in reducing the state's AFDC caseload. MinnesotaCare provides low-cost health insurance with affordable co-payments and premiums to 94,000 families with incomes up to 275 percent of the federal poverty line. Because help paying for health coverage no longer depends on families with sick children having little or no income, the state estimates that as of April 1996, 4,300 fewer families were on AFDC due to MinnesotaCare, with a net saving of $2.1 million a month.

(For more information, contact Mike Warner at CAP, 518-474-9307; or Jodie Eversman at MFIP, 612-297-5978.)

Opportunities to Help Children

If all American families with children are to achieve adequate incomes, there must be a renewal of a pro-family partnership among parents, business, and government. Parents must work hard to provide for their families and take advantage of education and other opportunities to better their own lives and their children's. Business must provide family-supporting wages and benefits, and must expand opportunities for young workers to enter and advance in the workplace. Government must ensure that parents have the tools they need (including education and training, child care, family health coverage, and transportation) to compete successfully in the twenty-first century economy, and must provide protections against poverty when work is not possible. Such a partnership is essential if we are to restore rather than erode the economic security of the American family.

✦ Most pressing in 1997, Congress and the President must remedy some of the aspects of the new welfare law that are most likely to worsen poverty. Urgently needed are changes to encourage education and training for parents, to protect children from destitution when time limits run out, and to undo the drastic cuts in benefits for legal immigrants and the deep reductions in food stamps (see Welfare chapter).

✦ States must use their new flexibility to design cash aid and work programs that give parents opportunities to get training and find family-supporting jobs, and that protect children from poverty. States now have the option to build poverty-fighting programs that imagi-

natively combine initiatives for job creation, job training and education, state minimum-wage increases, child care, health coverage, child support enforcement, unemployment insurance reforms, income supplements, and basic cash assistance. For states to make the choices necessary to pull large numbers of families out of poverty, strong and sustained political leadership will be necessary, with a willingness to spend state dollars to take on responsibilities abdicated by the federal government.

✦ Working families must be assured that work pays. The federal, state, and local governments should continue to increase the minimum wage until it again reaches the level at which a full-time, year-round job lifts at least a small family out of poverty. Businesses must do their part, by paying family-supporting wages and benefits, and by making advance payments of the EITC readily available to eligible employees. When low-wage work plus child support are not enough to make ends meet, states should supply income supplements that do not count against the welfare law's time limits.

✦ Unemployment compensation must be reconfigured to help more workers suffering from short-term unemployment, because many more jobs today than in previous years are part-time, temporary, or both, and workers with unstable earnings often do not qualify for unemployment. Only one in 10 mothers on welfare who has worked ever qualifies for unemployment compensation. If more could qualify, they would be far less likely to need welfare.

✦ Congress should not pass tax credits that would worsen both the deficit and income inequality, and that offer no help to low- and moderate-income families working to rise out of or stay out of poverty.

✦ All children need the support of both parents. States must implement the new child support enforcement provisions aggressively, and businesses should cooperate with efforts to collect child support from their employees. States also should mount child support assurance demonstration projects—making regular payments to children and then collecting the sums due from absent parents—so children do not suffer from sporadic collections.

✦ Employers must respond better to the needs of parents, through improved parental leave policies and flexible or part-time work schedules, and by providing child care help.

Health

The erosion of private, employer-based insurance coverage for American children of working parents is threatening their chances of getting a healthy start in life. Although Medicaid has been expanded over the past decade to cover many additional, mostly poor, children, the loss of private health coverage in working families with incomes above the poverty level has outdistanced Medicaid's growth. As a result, the number of uninsured children has risen from 8.2 million in 1987 to 9.8 million in 1995.

By far, the majority of these children have parents who are "playing by the rules": Nearly nine out of 10 have a working parent, and almost two-thirds have a parent who works full-time, year-round. But the parents' incomes are too high to qualify for Medicaid, their jobs don't provide employer-paid insurance coverage for their families, and they cannot afford to pay the high cost of premiums for family health insurance coverage.

Millions of additional American children were spared the loss of insurance in 1996, however, when Congress failed in its efforts to block-grant and deeply cut funding for Medicaid. Although the final welfare legislation did cut health coverage for many children with disabilities and for legal immigrants, it did not fundamentally alter Medicaid or withdraw that program's guarantee of health care coverage for low-income Americans, including one in four children, half of Black children, children with serious disabilities, and a large proportion of newborns.

At the same time, by enacting three limited measures to improve access to health coverage and the quality of health care, Congress showed it can pass incremental and bipartisan health reform. A few states, meanwhile, have been moving aggressively to insure more children, and many states have taken modest steps to protect consumers who are enrolled in managed care plans.

Data released in 1996 show improvements in some key areas of child health, most notably in protecting children from vaccine-preventable diseases (through the federal Vaccines for Children program and other important initiatives) and continued progress in maternal and child health for Black Americans. Despite these advances, many of the nation's maternal and child health goals for the year 2000 (in such areas as low birthweight) remain out of reach, and the health of America's children continues to lag behind that of children in most other industrialized nations.

Health Insurance Coverage for Children

In both 1994 and 1995, approximately 10 million U.S. children (one in seven) had no health insurance throughout the year—the highest numbers ever reported by the U.S. Census Bureau. Seven of 10 uninsured children are White, and six of 10 live in two-parent families. Millions more children lack health insurance for many months during the year, but not year-round.

Since 1989, the number of children lacking private coverage has risen by an average of 1.2 million each year—almost 3,300 more children a day, or one child every 26 seconds—because more workers are in jobs that either provide no health insurance benefits or require employees to pay un-affordable amounts for family coverage. In 1993, more than three-quarters of employees at medium and large companies had to pay some or all of the cost of family health insurance provided through their employers; in 1980, the proportion was less than half. If recent trends continue, by the year 2000, 40 percent of children will lack private coverage. As recently as 1989, only 26 percent lacked such coverage.

According to the most recent data from the Health Insurance Association of America, the total cost of family health coverage in 1992 averaged $4,560 to $5,040 per year. The U.S. Bureau of Labor Statistics reports that in 1993, employees of medium and large companies themselves paid an average of $1,300 a year for family coverage. Employees of small companies were even worse off: In 1994, they paid an average of $1,900 per year out of their own pockets for such coverage. For many moderate-income working families living from paycheck to paycheck, these costs are unaf-fordable—and their children are uninsured.

Many other working parents with uninsured children—part-time and temporary workers, the self-employed, independent contractors, and many employees of small businesses and service-sector companies—have employers that do not offer *any* health insurance. They face even higher insurance costs, because they don't have access to the discounts insurers offer large employers or to the partial premium payments some employers make.

The human costs of children's lack of health coverage are high: Study after study has shown that children and adults lacking health insurance are more likely than those with insurance to report poorer health, to see doctors less often (even when they are sick), to go without preventive care, and to turn to emergency rooms when they need treat-ment. Seven of 10 uninsured children live in fami-lies with incomes below 200 percent of poverty ($31,138 for a family of four in 1995). Many such families must choose between paying the full cost of prescriptions and doctor visits for uninsured children and paying for other basic family needs, including food and utility bills. Often uninsured children do not receive the regular check-ups that would spot problems early and permit prompt, cost-effective treatment. Uninsured children are only half as likely as other children to have a regular source of health care. Care is sometimes delayed when children are sick, with parents hop-ing that no harm results. According to the 1987

- In 1995, 9.8 million children (one in seven) had no health insurance.

- Since 1989, the number of children without private health insurance has risen each year by an average of 1.2 million.

- Eighty-eight percent of uninsured children have a working parent; 64 percent have a parent who works full-time, year-round.

- By 1994–1995, 75 percent of all 2-year-olds were fully immunized, up from 55 percent in 1992.

- In 1994, only 80.2 percent of babies were born to mothers who had received early (first-trimester) prenatal care, the infant mortality rate was 8.0 deaths per 1,000 live births, and 7.3 percent of newborns were born at low birthweight (less than 5 pounds, 8 ounces).

National Medical Expenditure Survey, one-third of uninsured children with two or more ear infections, and a majority of uninsured children with asthma, did not see a doctor during the entire year. Many uninsured children are hospitalized for asthma when they could have seen a doctor instead, and many with untreated ear infections suffer permanent hearing loss.

Perhaps less obvious, but no less damaging, are the educational, social, and economic costs to the children who lack health insurance, and to the nation. Children who are unnecessarily ill can miss days, weeks, or even months of school, and their parents can miss significant periods of work. A child who cannot see the blackboard well and whose parents cannot afford a visit to the eye doctor or eyeglasses cannot learn up to his or her potential. Uninsured pregnant women without adequate prenatal care are more likely to deliver babies with dangerously low birthweight, and the average hospital costs for a low-birthweight baby are 10 times the cost of prenatal care.

Congress in 1996 came close to adding huge numbers of children and pregnant women to the ranks of the uninsured, by attempting twice to destroy Medicaid—the public health insurance system for low-income families with children, preg-

nant women, seniors, and people with disabilities. Under current law, Medicaid covers most poor children, and coverage for *all* poor children—in working and non-working families—is being phased in. Medicaid's Early and Periodic Screening, Diagnosis, and Treatment (EPSDT) benefit guarantees all children in the program comprehensive health services when needed. But the congressional majority proposed repealing Medicaid, replacing it with a block grant, and drastically cutting projected funding levels.

The block grant would have left it up to each state to decide which seniors, people with disabilities, children, and parents to cover, and what services to give them—with vastly reduced funds that could not increase during recessions, when more families need help to get insurance. At least 12 million people, including 6 million children, were projected to lose health care coverage, even under optimistic scenarios of state responses to cuts in federal funding. President Clinton vetoed the attempt to block-grant Medicaid. While Congress and the White House debated which Medicaid cuts would be included in 1996 legislation, children's advocates and others maintained pressure on Congress and the President to reject the block grant. Ultimately, destruction of America's health

PARENTS OF UNINSURED CHILDREN WORK

Nearly *nine of 10 uninsured children have at least one parent who works. Almost two-thirds of these parents work full-time, year-round.*

Work status of parents of uninsured children, 1995

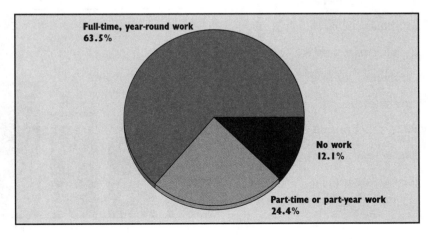

Full-time, year-round work
63.5%

No work
12.1%

Part-time or part-year work
24.4%

Source: U.S. Census Bureau, *Current Population Survey*, March 1996. Calculations by Children's Defense Fund.

safety net was removed from the final version of the welfare bill—a great victory for advocates of health care for children, pregnant women, parents, seniors, and people with disabilities.

Medicaid also was preserved for most of the millions of families that will lose cash benefits under the new welfare law: As a general rule, states must provide Medicaid to children and parents who *would have* qualified for Aid to Families with Dependent Children (AFDC) under the rules in effect in July 1996. However, the law's narrower definitions of disability mean that, among the estimated 250,000 to 315,000 children losing Supplemental Security Income (SSI) assistance, as many as 48,000 also could lose Medicaid coverage. And many hundreds of thousands of children will be among the *legal* immigrants faced with loss of Medicaid, SSI, food stamps, or cash welfare, under the new law. Immigrants already in the country when the law was enacted cannot receive Medicaid except for medical emergencies, unless their state opts to provide the coverage. Most immigrants arriving in this country after the law's adoption will not be able to receive Medicaid (except for emergency care) until five years after their entry. And after that, there are further barriers to their eligibility (see Welfare chapter).

In another important Medicaid development, the program's spending during 1996 grew by about 3 percent. This low rate of growth culminated an ongoing, dramatic slowdown in Medicaid cost increases, which averaged 22.4 percent a year from 1988 through 1992, and 9.5 percent a year from 1992 through 1995. The slowdown in Medicaid growth resulted from many factors, including limits on aggressive methods states previously used to evade the requirement of spending state dollars to match federal Medicaid funds; slower enrollment growth among families with children; slower medical inflation generally; and increased managed care enrollment.

Earlier in 1996, the Congressional Budget Office (CBO) had forecast annual increases of nearly 10 percent in Medicaid spending, buoying interest on Capitol Hill in aggressively cutting back the program. In January 1997, CBO revised its estimate and now projects an average annual growth rate of 7.7 percent from 1996 to 2002. At the federal level, slower spending growth should ease pressure for large Medicaid cuts and block grants, although other limits on the program and weakening of federal safeguards will be part of the budget debate in 1997. At the state level, slower Medicaid growth makes child health coverage expansions

CHILDREN WITHOUT PRIVATE INSURANCE

*L*ack of private health insurance among children has risen significantly since 1989. If current trends continue, in the year 2000 four of every 10 children will be without private coverage.

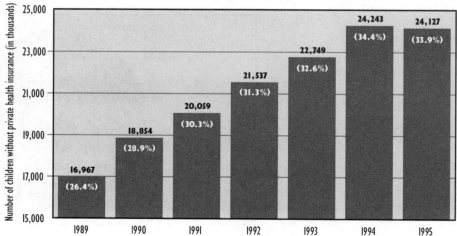

Children without private health insurance, 1989–1995 (in thousands)

Year	Number (in thousands)	Percentage
1989	16,967	(26.4%)
1990	18,854	(28.9%)
1991	20,059	(30.3%)
1992	21,537	(31.3%)
1993	22,749	(32.6%)
1994	24,243	(34.4%)
1995	24,127	(33.9%)

Note: Percentages shown are percentages of all children who lacked private health insurance in that year.
Source: U.S. Census Bureau, *Current Population Survey*, March 1990 through 1996.

more feasible, particularly when coupled with state budget surpluses, the possibility of targeted tax increases (such as Massachusetts' tobacco tax), and the availability of federal matching funds through Medicaid for middle-income as well as poor children.

Not all congressional health work in 1996 focused on Medicaid. A significant bipartisan incremental health reform measure, the Health Insurance Portability Act, limited insurance companies' ability to deny coverage of children and adults with health problems (known as "pre-existing conditions"). Insurers cannot refuse to cover medical problems of most newborn or newly adopted children, refuse to cover treatment for pre-existing conditions of other children or adults after they have had one year of continuous insurance coverage (even from multiple sources), or refuse to renew a family's plan because of a family member's health problems. The act also protects families from losing insurance when a worker leaves or is laid off from a job that had provided group coverage, requiring insurance companies to offer individual coverage. The bill has limitations, though: Insurance companies still can charge more to groups and individuals with high health costs, and the legislation does nothing to help people unable to afford insurance premiums.

At the state level, 1996 saw more initiatives to cover uninsured children. Massachusetts and New York made significant efforts to provide health insurance to large numbers of uninsured children, as a number of other states have done in recent years. With Gov. George E. Pataki taking the lead, New York extended to 13- to 18-year-olds its state-funded Child Health Plus program, which helps working families buy private health insurance for children. The move will more than double program enrollment, from 104,000 children to 251,000 children over the next two to three years. The state also expanded covered benefits greatly, adding inpatient care. Massachusetts, likewise, passed landmark legislation (see page 30) that will extend health coverage to at least 125,000 of the state's 160,000 previously uninsured children.

Immunization Gains

Immunization rates have improved rapidly and significantly, with related reductions in vaccine-preventable diseases. Nationally, 75 percent of 2-year-olds were fully immunized by the period of mid-1994 through the first half of

---

CHILD HEALTH COVERAGE: BEST AND WORST STATES

Percentage of children without health insurance

The percentage of children lacking health insurance varies greatly by state— from 6.7 percent in Minnesota to 24.7 percent in New Mexico.

Best states			Worst states		
Rank			Rank		
1.	Minnesota	6.7%	51.	New Mexico	24.7%
2.	Wisconsin	6.8	50.	Texas	22.7
3.	Vermont	7.5	49.	Oklahoma	22.6
4.	Hawaii	8.0	48.	Arizona	20.2
5.	Michigan	8.3	47.	Louisiana	19.9
6.	North Dakota	8.7	46.	Arkansas	19.0
7.	Massachusetts	9.0	45.	Nevada	18.7
8.	Nebraska	9.1	44.	California	18.3
9.	Washington	9.3	43.	Mississippi	17.7
10.	Ohio	9.4	42.	Florida	17.1
10.	South Dakota	9.4			
10.	Alaska	9.4			

Note: Percentages reflect the most recent reliable data from 1993–1995. Three years of data are averaged because of small sample sizes in many states. The full list includes the 50 states and Washington, D.C.

Source: U.S. Census Bureau, *Current Population Survey*, March 1994 through March 1996. Calculations by Children's Defense Fund.

1995, according to data released in 1996. As recently as 1992, just 55 percent were fully immunized. This striking increase was accompanied by a nearly two-fifths reduction in all vaccine-preventable illnesses except pertussis among children younger than 5, from 1993 to 1996. Because of less effective vaccine and parental concerns about the vaccine's side effects, pertussis alone has proved resistant to immunization efforts, with disease rates rising slightly between 1994 and 1996 as part of a typical cycle for the illness.

At the state level, more recent data indicate that immunization rate gains are continuing. According to state health officials responding to a Children's Defense Fund survey:

✦ In Illinois, immunization rates rose from 62 percent in 1995 to about 72 percent in 1996.
✦ Oklahoma's rates rose from 63 percent in 1993 to 74 percent in 1996.

Parents became more aware of the need for vaccinating their children after declining immunization rates in the 1980s culminated in the 1989–1991 measles epidemic, which involved 55,000 cases, 11,000 hospitalizations, and 130 deaths. As a result of the epidemic, many government bodies at all levels stepped up parent educa-

tion and outreach efforts, education of providers to take full advantage of opportunities to immunize children, immunization registries that pinpoint children who are missing vaccinations, and extension of clinic hours so employed parents could get their children vaccinated after work and on weekends.

Congress and the Clinton Administration significantly expanded efforts on all these fronts and also enacted the Vaccines for Children (VFC) program in 1993 to help uninsured, Medicaid-eligible, and Native American children get vaccinated during routine visits to their regular doctors. The price of all required vaccines for preschool children had risen from $28 in the early 1980s to $270 by 1994, before VFC first took effect. Concerned about families' inability to afford these costs and the inadequacy of Medicaid reimbursements for vaccines, many private doctors referred to public clinics many of their uninsured patients, their patients covered by Medicaid, and children from the more than three out of five privately insured families whose policies didn't cover immunizations. Parents already facing a complex schedule of required immunizations—involving 15 vaccinations before age 2 alone—and already forced to take time off work for each pediatric appointment, were asked

IMMUNIZATIONS UP, PREVENTABLE DISEASES DOWN

*R*ates of vaccine-preventable childhood illnesses have fallen more than one-third since 1993, as a result of greatly improved immunization rates since the early 1990s.

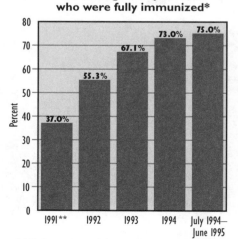

Percentage of 2-year-olds who were fully immunized*

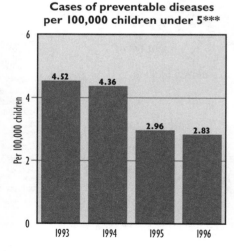

Cases of preventable diseases per 100,000 children under 5**

* Includes vaccines and dosages recommended in 1991 for full immunization. Taking into account the new Hib vaccine, introduced after 1992, the mid-1994 to mid-1995 immunization rate would be 73 percent.
**Survey methods used to obtain 1991 data were slightly different from those used in other years, so data are not directly comparable.
***Excludes pertussis because of strong cyclical variations; 1996 rate is based on provisional CDC data.
Source: U.S. Centers for Disease Control and Prevention (CDC).

to make still more trips to other, often unfamiliar health care providers. These public clinics, overwhelmed with referrals, often had long lines and waiting lists, and many even ran out of vaccine.

VFC helps solve these problems by purchasing all recommended vaccines and placing them, free of charge, in the offices of private doctors and in clinics for uninsured children and Medicaid-covered children. (Children with private insurance that does not cover vaccinations can be immunized through VFC, but only at certain health clinics.) Several studies show dramatically improved immunization rates when children receive immunizations and other well-child care from the same provider.

VFC also speeds up the routine use of new vaccines. In the past, the cost of new vaccines, which often are the most expensive, slowed their acceptance and general use, so the vaccines did not reach children quickly. Today, when a vaccine is recommended for universal use by the National Vaccine Advisory Committee of the Centers for Disease Control and Prevention, VFC coverage speeds its dissemination, as it did for the newly approved chicken pox vaccine (varicella).

VFC now is operating in all 50 states and has enrolled more than 84,000 providers, 62,000 of whom are private physicians. Attesting to this strategy's effectiveness, 28 states have used their own funds to apply VFC's approach to additional children—either all children in the state or children with private health insurance not covering vaccinations—so more children can be vaccinated in the offices of their regular doctors. VFC has become an "integral component of our efforts to immunize 90 percent of all 2-year-olds against preventable diseases by the year 2000," according to John Lumpkin, president of the Association of State and Territorial Health Officials.

The efforts to improve immunization rates among young children have paid off: In 1996, the rate of measles among children under 5 fell to less than one case per 100,000 children, from an average of 44 cases per 100,000 in 1989 through 1991 and an average of seven cases per 100,000 from 1980 through 1988, before the epidemic. In 1996, the rates of mumps, *Haemophilus influenzae*, congenital rubella, diphtheria, and tetanus among young children all were at the lowest levels ever reported.

SURGEON GENERAL'S GOALS

Progress toward meeting the U.S. Surgeon General's maternal and child health goals for the year 2000

Indicator	Race	1991 Rate	1994 Rate	2000 Goal	Projected 2000 Rate	Projected Year Goal Reached
Infant mortality	Overall	8.9 infant deaths per 1,000 live births	8.0	7.0	6.2	1998
	Black	17.6	15.8	11.0	12.2	2002
Early prenatal care	Overall	76.2% of all births	80.2%	90%	88.2%	2002
	Black	61.9%	68.3%	90%	81.1%	2005
	Hispanic	61.0%	68.9%	90%	84.7%	2002
Low birthweight	Overall	7.1% of all births	7.3%	5%	7.7%	Never
	Black	13.6%	13.2%	9%	12.4%	2026

Notes: For Hispanics, the Surgeon General articulated a distinct goal only for early prenatal care. To project future numbers, this chart assumes a continuation of 1991–1994 trends. See Appendix for more refined, current data about a variety of racial and ethnic groups. Hispanics may be of any race.

Source: National Center for Health Statistics. Calculations by Children's Defense Fund.

Maternal and Child Health

The goal of immunizing 90 percent of American children is only one of a group of goals for improving child health set in 1990 by the U.S. Surgeon General for the nation to meet by the year 2000. As the table on page 27 shows, most of these goals will not be met on time, if 1991–1994 trends continue. Maternal and child health is improving overall, but not nearly quickly enough, particularly for Black children.

One important area that has improved, albeit too slowly, is pregnant women's receipt of early prenatal care. In 1994, 80.2 percent of babies were born to mothers who had begun prenatal care in the first trimester of pregnancy, compared with 78.9 percent in 1993 and 75.8 percent in 1990. By contrast, the rate of early prenatal care had fallen between 1980 and 1990. Of equal significance, recent gains have been nearly across-the-board: From 1991 through 1994, early prenatal care rates increased each year for 14 of 15 racial and ethnic groups tracked by the Census Bureau.

Overall infant mortality (deaths of babies before their first birthday) also improved in 1994 (the latest year for which final data are available), continuing its three-decade decline; 31,710 babies died, for a rate of 8.0 per 1,000 live births, compared with 8.4 in 1993.

However, the overall percentage of babies born at low birthweight (less than 5.5 pounds) worsened again in 1994, reaching its highest level in almost 20 years. Nearly 300,000 babies, or 7.3 percent, were born at low birthweight, compared with 7.2 percent in 1993. Babies born at low birthweight are at greater risk of death and of disabilities, including developmental delays, cerebral palsy, and seizure disorders. While the rate rose for White babies and remained constant for Hispanics, the low-birthweight rate once again declined among Black babies.

For Black families there is additional good news: Every key indicator of maternal and child health has improved each year since 1991, and almost all have improved every year since 1990. This represents a dramatic change in direction from the 1980s, when every major indicator of maternal and child health worsened for Black children in all but two years.

The maternal and child health improvements suggest that the combination of better medical technology, Medicaid's expanded coverage of prenatal care and care for infants, and other public and private initiatives at all levels is bearing fruit. However, the persistence of large, although slightly narrowed, gaps in health status between Black newborns and others confirms what is known from the Surgeon General's goals: We have a long way to go.

Black babies still die at more than twice the rate of White babies (15.8 deaths per 1,000 live births, compared with 6.6), and are more likely to die in infancy than babies in some developing countries. If babies born to Black mothers died at the same rate as babies born to White mothers, almost 6,000 fewer Black babies would have died in 1994. The Black low-birthweight rate (13.2 percent) is more than twice that of Whites (6.2 percent).

Equally telling is the poor U.S. international standing on maternal and child health. Based on UNICEF data, the U.S. infant mortality rate ranks eighteenth among industrialized countries. Only Portugal does worse. If our infant mortality rate were as low as Japan's, more than 15,000 U.S. babies who died before their first birthdays in 1994 would still be alive.

Quality of Care

Insurance is vital to protecting the health of children and families, but the *quality* of care ultimately determines whether their health needs are met. The continuing shift to managed care from fee-for-service insurance creates both risks of harm and opportunities to improve the quality of care for children.

Managed care plans, such as Health Maintenance Organizations (HMOs), generally involve a provider network that is paid a set, per capita ("capitated") fee in advance for providing most or all health care for a beneficiary. Non-emergency hospitalization and referrals to specialists often require prior approval from a primary care case manager.

In large part because many states have received federal waivers to override Medicaid freedom of choice rules, among Medicaid families with children the number of people enrolled in managed care more than tripled from 1992 (3.6 million beneficiaries) to 1995 (11.6 million beneficiaries—one-third of all Medicaid enrollment). Private-sector use of managed care also has been increasing. Altogether, more than 113 million Americans were enrolled in some form of managed care in 1995, according to KMPG Peat Marwick. The simultaneous movement of low-income and middle-class families into managed care leads to the possibility of safeguards that help *both* sets of families, and are likely to have more political support and staying power than safeguards for low-income families alone.

A majority of states took modest action in 1996 to protect people enrolled in managed care plans, and most of the safeguards enacted will affect the care children receive. Several states outlawed "gag rules"—clauses in managed care contracts that forbid doctors and other providers to give patients information about managed care plans, reimbursements, and alternative treatment possibilities. Some states also gave women the right of direct access to obstetricians/gynecologists, without requiring prior approval from primary care "gatekeepers." Between mid-1995 and mid-1996,

12 states passed laws or regulations aimed at improving managed care consumers' access to emergency care, following reports of troubling problems with patients suffering long delays in emergency rooms waiting for HMOs to authorize admission.

In other steps important to consumers, the Health Care Financing Administration (HCFA) finalized regulations that require Medicaid and Medicare managed care plans to disclose and limit incentive payments made to physicians for curbing referrals, and to conduct patient satisfaction surveys. HCFA also released several documents with useful recommendations and questions about Medicaid managed care, including *Integrating EPSDT and Managed Care* and *Medicaid Managed Care Monitoring Guide.*

Additional modest steps were provoked by complaints about managed care but apply to other insurers as well. Under the federal Newborns' and Mothers' Health Protection Act, health insurers that cover hospitalization for childbirth must cover stays of at least 48 hours after a normal vaginal birth and 96 hours after a Caesarean-section birth, beginning January 1, 1998. To cut costs, many insurers had limited their coverage of hospital stays after deliveries to half these periods, resulting in babies re-hospitalized because of dehydration and jaundice. Many state legislatures had passed similar bills. Another modest, but impor-

AIDS and HIV Infection

◆ Since 1991, roughly 1,000 children and young people under 25 have died each year from AIDS. Many adults who die of AIDS acquired HIV as teens.

◆ Almost 30,000 children and young people under 25 have been diagnosed with AIDS, and about 10,000 have died of AIDS since 1981.

◆ Although children and teens represent less than 2 percent of all AIDS cases,

AIDS has become the sixth leading cause of death among 1- to 4-year-olds.

◆ Treatment of HIV-infected pregnant women has helped reduce the rate of AIDS transmission to newborns by 27 percent since 1992.

◆ Among 15- to 24-year-olds, in 1994 AIDS was the sixth leading cause of death overall, but the third leading cause of death of Black females and the fourth leading cause for Black males.

tant, improvement made at the federal level in 1996 bars health insurance plans provided by employers of more than 50 workers from imposing lower annual and lifetime limits for mental health services (if such coverage is provided) than for physical health care.

Despite progress, there still is a long way to go to protect consumers—especially children and low-income consumers, who have the least ability to protect themselves—in the new world of managed care. There must be more efforts, for example, to hold managed care plans accountable for providing the services children need, including the comprehensive services that Medicaid guarantees; to assure that providers are accessible and provide high-quality care; and to prevent new financial arrangements from creating strong incentives to deny essential care to patients.

Health Reform in Massachusetts

Broad-based support was the key to victory for Massachusetts health care reform for children in June 1996. The legislation, passed with strong bipartisan legislative backing that overrode Gov. William Weld's veto, likely will make Massachusetts the state with the lowest rate of uninsured children.

The new law expands the state's Medicaid program to provide comprehensive coverage to children 12 and younger in families with incomes under 200 percent of the poverty level ($25,960 for a family of three in 1996). Uninsured children through age 18 with family incomes of less than 400 percent of poverty ($51,920 for a three-person family), and who are ineligible for Medicaid, will receive primary and preventive care through the state's Children's Medical Security Plan. Their hospital care will be covered through the state's Free Care Pool. When the law is fully implemented, at least 125,000 of the state's 160,000 uninsured children will have health coverage. The expansions are financed through increased federal Medicaid funding and a cigarette tax hike of 25 cents a pack.

Massachusetts provides a good model of how to extend health insurance to more children. The legislation improved health coverage for a broad span of people—seniors, people with disabilities, and uninsured adults, as well as children. Accordingly, it attracted a broad range of support. Backers included business leaders, teachers' unions, tobacco control advocates, uninsured adults, senior citizens, health insurers, health care providers, children's advocates, and disability rights groups.

Business was brought into the fold because key business leaders were shocked when informed of the large number of uninsured children in the state. Business support was particularly strong because the law also repealed a mandate that employers provide health insurance, which was enacted a decade earlier but never implemented.

Lead Poisoning

Lead poisoning in children can cause serious, sometimes irreversible, damage, including cognitive and hearing impairment, convulsions, coma, and even death. New research also links elevated lead levels to various forms of antisocial behavior. Children with higher bone-lead levels than other children showed significantly more attention problems, aggression, and delinquent behavior, according to a report in the February 1996 issue of *JAMA: The Journal of the American Medical Association*. If the findings are applicable to all U.S. children, the report said, "the contribution of lead to delinquent behavior would be substantial....Environmental lead exposure, a preventable occurrence, should be included when considering the many factors contributing to delinquent behavior."

The law appealed to seniors because it expanded coverage of prescription drugs for low-income senior citizens. People with disabilities and adults with incomes up to 133 percent of the poverty level gained health coverage through a Medicaid waiver.

The legislation's primary opponents were the tobacco industry, Weld (who wanted to cover children without a tobacco tax increase), and a small number of groups unhappy about the employer-mandate repeal. Supporters considered the increased health coverage for children and others well worth repeal of the mandate, which they believed had no serious prospects of implementation in the foreseeable future.

Rob Restuccia, executive director of the Boston-based Health Care for All, says other states pushing for expanded health coverage should create similarly broad-based coalitions, put a human face on the problem of uninsured children by mobilizing children and families most affected, link the needs of children and senior citizens in one bill, and work to expand existing health coverage programs.

(For further information, contact Allison Staton at Health Care for All, 617-350-7279, ext. 110.)

Opportunities to Help Children

Major efforts are likely in the 105th Congress, as well as many state legislatures, to expand health coverage to insure America's nearly 10 million uninsured children. As these efforts go forward, it will be important to avoid large, new cuts to the Medicaid program, which now covers one in four children. The protections Medicaid provides eligible children, parents, and pregnant women, and the services covered, including EPSDT, are essential to the nation's health.

But it also is time to address the problem of the one in seven children with no insurance. Every segment of society has a responsibility to help children receive necessary health care. Parents should use every opportunity to buy health insurance and provide care for their children. Employers must renew their willingness to provide workers with family health coverage and other family-supporting benefits. They should stop dropping coverage of children and pay the premiums for family coverage. States should ensure that all eligible children are enrolled in Medicaid, and should adopt good child health programs like those adopted in 1996 in New York and Massachusetts.

The federal government also must help working families obtain health insurance for their uninsured children. A child's chances of growing up healthy and strong should not depend on the state in which he or she happens to live.

Any initiative on children's health coverage must be effective, not cosmetic or symbolic, and should include certain basic principles:

✦ Uninsured children at least through age 18 and uninsured pregnant women should receive coverage for the full range of necessary services, including care required for children with special needs.

✦ Proposals should build on successful private, state, and federal efforts to help working families afford health insurance for their children; they must offer sufficient and timely assistance that realistically lets families obtain health coverage for their children.

✦ While there is broad consensus that working parents should help pay for their children's private insurance coverage, costs must be affordable, must be based on family income, and must allow *all* families to obtain coverage and seek care for their children.

Child Care and
Early Education

Major events in 1996 and ongoing national trends joined to place extraordinary new demands upon the nation's already over-burdened and underfunded child care and early education services.

✦ The new welfare law requires parents of all but the very youngest children to work, and their children will need child care during the work-day.

✦ Many parents already in low-wage jobs must have help paying for child care if they are to continue working and avoid welfare.

✦ And to build an economically strong future, America needs more high-quality child care to prepare its youngest and most vulnerable children to learn in school and succeed in adulthood.

Even before the demands that the 1996 wel-fare law will create, affordable and supportive child care is beyond the reach of too many American families. The lack of adequate public and private commitment to ensuring that children are safe, secure, and developing while their parents work is reflected in the vast underfunding of the nation's child care system and widespread neglect of quality of care. Every day, parents must debate whether to leave their children with older siblings still too young to care for them, or home alone after school, or in questionable but affordable care. Many face the question of whether to spend more for child care than they can afford or to give up on work. States and communities see waiting lists grow, and ponder whether to devote scarce dollars to helping families leave welfare or to keeping families off welfare, to making child care more affordable for families or to improving the quality of care children receive.

The welfare law will exacerbate these dilem-mas. Although child care funds added by the law were heralded as one of its positive aspects, the increase is not nearly sufficient to help all of the millions of families that will need child care if they are to move from welfare to work. In addition, the already-inadequate child care help for low-income working families that are trying to stay off welfare is in even greater jeopardy because of the law. Unless states increase their investments suffi-ciently—and there are several signs indicating they may not—communities will face an even larger gap between families' need for help in paying for good child care and the resources to ensure that it is available to them. And families will face more impossible choices.

Child Care and Early Education Essential to Meet National Goals

Helping families work and helping chil-dren get a strong start in school and in life are inextricable goals. Child care and early education assistance build the current and future work force, ensure that children get what they need to succeed, and enable families to support themselves.

The nation cannot put more of today's parents to work without providing them access to the af-fordable, stable, and decent child care that enables them to find and keep jobs. Care for even one young child can easily cost $4,000 a year. Many parents leaving welfare (as well as those trying to stay off welfare) have limited education and work experience, and will be in jobs that do not pay enough to cover the cost of child care on top of other necessities, such as rent, food, and clothing. Employer help with the costs of child care is fairly uncommon, and rare among low-wage jobs, which also tend to be less flexible about hours lost when child care arrangements fall through.

Child care that satisfies parents supports their ability to work. Evaluations of GAIN, the job-training program for welfare recipients in California, found that mothers who were worried about the safety of their children and who did not trust their providers were twice as likely to drop out of the job-training program as those who were satisfied with their child care.

A lack of reliable child care also can cause workers to lose time and be less productive at work. A 1991 study found that nearly one out of every six employed mothers reported losing some time from work during the previous month because of a failure in child care arrangements.

The development of the nation's economic and social future also requires that children be safe and be prepared to enter school ready to learn and succeed. The children of low-income working parents, including those leaving welfare, are extremely vulnerable. Their poverty or near-poverty places them at greater risk of educational failure, and their families and neighborhoods often cannot afford the "extras" that help wealthier children learn and develop. They need the boost provided by *good* child care and early education programs.

These are the very same children that the nation's governors and President Bush were concerned about in 1989, when they set the goal of ensuring that all children should enter school ready to learn by the year 2000 and stated that good early childhood programs are key to meeting this goal. But the November 1996 Goals Panel Report on the nation's progress toward this and other year 2000 education goals found that the large gap in preschool participation between 3- to 5-year-olds in high- and low-income families did not shrink between 1991 and 1996. The failure to give children early learning experiences is having adverse consequences for school readiness. According to the Carnegie Corporation's *Years of Promise: A Comprehensive Strategy for America's Children*, kindergarten teachers estimate that one in three children enters the classroom unprepared to meet the challenges of kindergarten.

Facts & Figures

+ About 7.7 million children younger than 5 are being cared for by someone other than their parents while their mothers work. Fifty-nine percent are in day care centers and family day care homes.

+ Thirty-eight states and the District of Columbia had waiting lists of low-income families needing child care assistance in 1994, often with tens of thousands of children.

+ Only about one in three eligible children attends Head Start.

+ A year of child care for just one young child can cost a family $4,000.

+ Two-thirds of states spend more than 10 times as much on corrections and prisons as on child care and early education.

Child development experts tell us that during the first three years of life, children learn—or fail to learn—how to get along with others, how to resolve disputes peaceably, how to use language as a tool of learning and persuasion, and how to explore the world without fear. Recent research underscores the importance of this period: Brain development that occurs during the first three years is more extensive, is more vulnerable to environmental influences, and has a longer-term impact than previously realized. Other studies have shown that high-quality child care can make a difference for low-income children. The Packard Foundation, in *Long-Term Outcomes of Early Childhood Programs,* reported that children in high-quality programs are less likely, later on, to need special education or be retained a grade, and are less likely to engage in juvenile delinquency and other antisocial behavior as they grow up. Programs that begin earlier in a child's life are the most effective.

Unmet Need

Despite the importance of child care and early education, our society's financial commitment to assistance for them is terribly inadequate, leading to problems in supply, affordability, and quality. Low-income working families that are not on welfare face particular difficulties obtaining the help they need to stay employed. In 1995, 38 states and the District of Columbia had waiting lists of low-income working families needing child care assistance. Waiting lists are often overwhelming:

◆ Texas had more than 35,000 children on its waiting list in 1995, with a wait for help as long as two years.

◆ Illinois had approximately 20,000 children on its waiting list. Priority was given to teen parents, children needing protective services, children with special needs, and a handful of other categories. Families outside those categories probably never will make it off the waiting list.

◆ The waiting list in Florida recently reached almost 28,000—the highest number since 1991.

Head Start, the federally funded early childhood development program that recognizes the importance of supporting vulnerable children and their families with enriched services, serves only about one in three eligible children. In ad-

WHO'S WATCHING THE CHILDREN?

Of the 7.7 million children younger than 5 who were cared for by someone other than a parent in 1993 while their mothers worked, 59 percent were in child care centers and family day care homes.

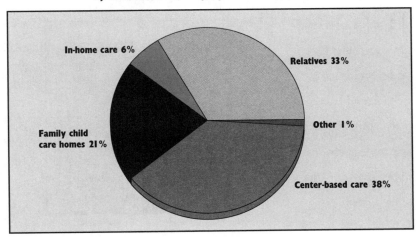

Child care arrangements used for preschoolers by families with employed mothers, 1993

In-home care 6%
Relatives 33%
Other 1%
Center-based care 38%
Family child care homes 21%

Source: U.S. Census Bureau, *Current Population Reports,* No. P70-53, "Who's Minding Our Preschoolers?"

dition, only about 30 percent of programs operate all day, year-round. While some states, including Ohio, Georgia, and Kentucky, are investing significant resources in prekindergarten or Head Start programs, many states invest relatively little or nothing in early childhood education services.

As a consequence of these inadequate investments, in 1995 only 45 percent of 3- to 5-year-olds from low-income families were enrolled in early care and education, compared with 71 percent from high-income families.

In many parts of the country, child care simply isn't available. Such gaps leave the country ill-prepared for the surge in demand that the welfare law will cause. One recent study found that nine of 55 counties in West Virginia had no child care centers. Similar gaps were found in Illinois. Other studies have found that child care is particularly hard to find in low-income communities. According to the U.S. Department of Education:

✦ Public schools in low-income communities were far less likely to offer prekindergarten programs (16 percent) than were schools in more affluent areas (almost one-third).

✦ Schools in low-income areas were much less likely to offer the extended-day and enriched programs that can help keep children safe after school and help them stay out of trouble. In 1993, only one-third of the schools in low-income neighborhoods offered such programs, compared with 52 percent of schools in more affluent areas.

The financial condition of many child care providers and the low pay for child care workers also threaten the supply. A 1996 report on the Wisconsin child care work force found that licensed family child care providers had an average net income of just $8,344 annually. Certified providers, subject to less training and fewer requirements, earned $5,132 after expenses. Almost half of the providers surveyed said they didn't know how much longer they would continue to operate their family child care businesses. Budget cuts in the Child and Adult Care Food Program (see Food and Nutrition chapter) will make it even harder for these family child care programs to stay in business.

CHILD CARE, PRESCHOOL, AND INCOME

Higher-income children are more likely to be enrolled in preschool, and their neighborhood schools are more likely to provide before- and after-school care.

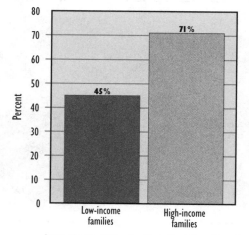

Percent of 3- to 5-year-olds enrolled in preschool, by income, 1995

Source: National Education Goals Panel, *Data Volume for the National Education Goals Report, Volume 1: National Data, 1995.*

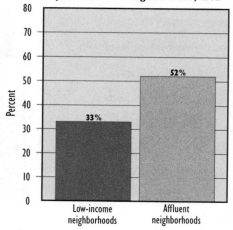

Percent of public schools offering extended-day (before- and after-school) and enrichment programs, by affluence of neighborhood, 1993

Source: U.S. Department of Education, *The Condition of Education: 1993.*

Many Children in Poor-Quality Care

When families can find child care, too often the care is of poor quality. According to the Carnegie Corporation, child care and early education services "have so long been neglected that they now constitute some of the worst services for children in Western society." A national study on center-based care found that most such care is "poor to mediocre, with almost half of the infants and toddlers in rooms having less than minimal quality." Another national study found equally alarming patterns in family child care homes, to which many families entrust their younger, more vulnerable children. This study rated one-third of the programs inadequate, which means their quality was low enough to actually harm children's development. Only 9 percent of the homes studied were rated as having good quality. The study also found that low-income and minority children were more likely than others to be in lower-quality programs.

The Carnegie *Years of Promise* report cites a forthcoming study by the Quality 2000 Initiative of Yale University's Bush Center in Child Development and Social Policy, which concludes that the care most children are in not only can "threaten their immediate health and safety, but also can compromise their long-term development."

Impact of 1996 Welfare Legislation

The new welfare law has major implications for the future of child care. It requires that adults participate in work activities within two years of receiving Temporary Assistance for Needy Families (TANF), unless they have children under 6 and cannot find affordable and appropriate child care. Adults receiving assistance for more than two months must work off their benefits through community-service jobs, unless their states opt out of this provision. And federal funds for most families have a lifetime limit of five years, regardless of whether the families are able to find work and the child care that makes work possible. Exemptions from these rules are limited. Millions of additional low-income parents will be struggling to enter and stay in the work force, many at wages too low to pay for subsistence needs and also pay for child care without assistance.

Under the old law, while funds for non-welfare working families with low incomes were inadequate, there was a guarantee of child care assistance for families on welfare and for one year for

PAYING FOR CHILD CARE

Child care consumes a much larger share of the budget of lower-income families. Among families paying for preschoolers' care, those with incomes under $14,400 a year (or $1,200 a month) devote one-quarter of their incomes to child care.

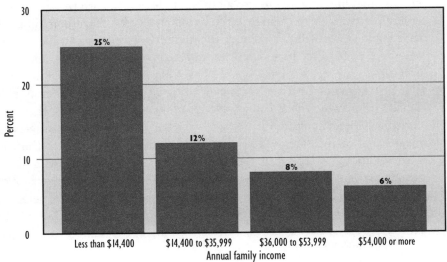

Percent of annual family income spent on child care for preschoolers, 1993

Percent (y-axis)

- Less than $14,400: 25%
- $14,400 to $35,999: 12%
- $36,000 to $53,999: 8%
- $54,000 or more: 6%

Annual family income

Source: U.S. Census Bureau, *Current Population Reports*, No. P70-52, "What Does it Cost to Mind Our Preschoolers?"

CHILD CARE AND EARLY EDUCATION

those transitioning off welfare. The new law ends these guarantees, pulls all the major funding streams into the Child Care and Development Block Grant, and replaces them with a fixed amount of funds.

Congress recognized that the availability of safe and affordable child care is key to the success of efforts to reform welfare, by including in the welfare law approximately $4 billion in new child care funds over six years. But the new law forces so many parents into the work force that this increase falls far short of what is needed to meet the new demand for child care generated by the law, much less to ensure that vulnerable children receive *good* care. The Congressional Budget Office estimates that the law provides $1.4 billion less than what is needed over six years for the child care necessary to meet the work requirements, even if states put up all of the state matching funds needed to obtain the new federal dollars.

But Congress structured the law in a way that makes it likely that the gap between what's needed and what's available will grow even wider:

✦ The new law requires states to come up with state matching funds to get the new federal dollars for child care. A 1996 Children's Defense Fund analysis of state efforts in 1994, *Who Cares? State Commitment to Early Care and Education*, suggests that many states will not do so: 20 states did not even provide enough matching money to use all of the federal funds available to them in 1994. It is likely that many states will not commit the greater resources needed to draw down the new federal funds.

✦ The new law cuts the Title XX Social Services Block Grant, which many states use for child care, by 15 percent after Fiscal Year 1997. This means that many states will have to come up with additional state funds just to maintain *current* service levels.

✦ The new law cuts spending on the Child and Adult Care Food Program (CACFP) by $2.3 billion over six years. These cuts (described in the Food and Nutrition chapter) will have a chilling effect on the supply of licensed and regulated family child care, because CACFP benefits have been a financial support and a major incentive for family child care providers to become licensed or regulated. CACFP also offers training and technical assistance to family child care providers, who work long hours in an isolating job with little support from their states or other community institutions. It is expected that the cuts will cause a substantial number of providers either to operate illegally or simply to stop providing child care services.

It is impossible to predict what states will do as a result of these shortfalls. But evidence from the *Who Cares?* report indicates that many states are already far behind in their commitment to provide child care and early education to families. The report found that:

✦ All states place child care and early education low on their list of priorities. Twenty-nine states spend less than 50 cents out of every $100 of state tax revenues on these important family supports. Two-thirds of the states spend more than 10 times as much on corrections and prisons as on child care and early education.

✦ State commitment varies enormously across the country; the 10 states with the greatest commitment allotted an average of 4.5 times as much, per child in the state, as the 10 states with the smallest commitment.

✦ State commitment reflects state "will" rather than "wallet." For example, Kentucky, North Carolina, and Oklahoma were among the *top* third of states in their commitment to child care and early education in 1994, yet were in the *lowest* third in personal income per capita. In contrast, Nevada and Virginia were both in the lowest third on financial commitment to child care and early education, but ranked eleventh and fourteenth from the top, respectively, on personal income per capita. There were 7,000 children in Nevada and 13,700 families in Virginia on waiting lists for child care assistance.

What Happens Next?

With child care funding, quality, and supply already inadequate, and massive new demands brewing, states face some very stark choices. States could choose to assure that all low-income families, whether on welfare or not, have access to child care assistance, and to ensure that the care all children receive is of high quality. There are limited signs that some state governments and other partners, including the business community, are moving forward. Rhode Island recently *guaranteed* child care assistance on a sliding scale to all families earning less than 185 percent of the federal poverty level (approximately $24,000 for a family of three). Recognizing the importance of supporting family child care providers, most of whom provide crucial services and earn very little, the state also made them eligible for free health care through Rhode Island Cares, the state's health plan for low-income families.

Florida's Child Care Partnership Act is an unusual three-way venture among the state, the business community, and parents. It guarantees up to $2 million of state funds (which must be matched by employers) to support child care subsidies for low-income working families.

A few states are making very significant investments in prekindergarten programs, so that their children can enter school ready to learn. Georgia, through leadership of Gov. Zell Miller, continues to expand its lottery-funded program, providing to all families with 4-year-olds a range of services and early education—in some cases for a full day. Similarly, Ohio, with Gov. George Voinovich's leadership, continues to make early childhood a high priority, moving toward using state money to provide full funding for Head Start, with a set-aside to help programs provide full-day, full-year services for families receiving TANF. The state estimates that by 1998, all eligible children who want a Head Start will be served by the combined federal and state Head Start funding and public prekindergarten funds. And Kentucky, as a result of its education reform efforts, is close to serving all eligible low-income 4-year-olds with its state prekindergarten and Head Start funds.

But there are clear indications that many states are considering shortsighted choices that would produce dire results for children and families, such as leaving working poor parents without the assistance they need, loosening standards for care, and changing policies to compromise child care quality and limit parents' child care choices.

Wisconsin, for one, plans to set parent fee policies so that parents who choose less expensive care will pay less in fees than parents who choose higher-quality care. And Virginia has proposed changing its licensing requirements to allow child care providers without training, high school diplomas, or GEDs to work with children, and to allow one caregiver to be responsible for 15 4-year-olds.

Allegheny County Early Childhood Initiative

Allegheny County in Pennsylvania has created an unprecedented public–private partnership that is in the early stage of expanding families' access to high-quality early care and education services. The Early Childhood Initiative (ECI) is designed to improve the futures of the poorest children, who are at greatest risk of school dropout, school failure, and juvenile delinquency.

ECI was sparked in October 1994, when the United Way of Allegheny County accepted an invitation from the Howard Heinz Endowment to develop and manage a community-wide initiative to address the downward spiral faced by many low-income children. A unique coalition of 80 business leaders, educators, parents, health care providers, and early childhood professionals met regularly in small clusters to discuss children's needs. Out of those meetings, ECI emerged, a five-year business plan was developed, and the coalition began mobilizing foundations and corporations. By the end of 1996, $16 million of the anticipated $59.4 million implementation cost had been raised from the private sector.

Eighty neighborhoods in Allegheny County, including many in Pittsburgh, are being asked to undertake a planning process, conducting surveys and focus groups to find out what kind of early care and education services would best serve families' needs, and then to submit individualized proposals to participate in ECI.

ECI funds will be used for everything from helping communities build new facilities, to rehabilitating existing Head Start classrooms, to helping family child care providers improve their environments for children. To ensure that services remain high-quality, teachers and caregivers will undergo more training in child development and early childhood education. Child-to-staff ratios will be low, so teachers can spend more individualized time with each child. And quality will be assessed continually by the United Way.

ECI seeks to enroll every eligible child under 6 in high-quality early childhood programs, including Head Start, preschools, and child care. Trained outreach workers will go door-to-door in public housing neighborhoods to identify eligible children. Initially, children in families with incomes up to the poverty level—$12,980 for a family of three in 1996—will be eligible for Head Start, and child care help will be available to working families earning up to 185 percent of the poverty line. ECI planners recommend gradually raising these eligibility levels by one-third. It is estimated that by 2002, ECI will serve 80 percent of the children in targeted neighborhoods—about 7,600 more children, double the number now served.

One key factor in ECI's momentum is that people who generally do not work together have joined forces. "ECI was a program whose time had come," says Mardi Isler, ECI director. "Business leaders realized that the work force of the future needed to be prepared with skills and training. Early childhood professionals knew that the current child care situation—where more than 1,000 children of working poor parents are on waiting lists to receive help with child care and where so many young children are not served by any program—wasn't working."

For the first 18 months, the United Way of Allegheny County will manage ECI and monitor all fundraising efforts. After that, responsibility for ECI will be transferred to a lead agency that will be identified by the end of 1997. To gauge the effectiveness of ECI, participating children will be tracked through the fifth grade—or through high school, if funding becomes available. It is hoped that by the year 2002, funding for ECI will come from re-programming local, state, and federal revenue already in the social service system.

(For more information, contact Mardi Isler at the United Way of Allegheny County, 412-456-6793.)

Opportunities to Help Children

A broad group of partners—including parents, businesses, community organizations, and federal, state, and local governments—must join together and expand their commitment to improving families' child care and early education options.

Financial commitment to child care and early education must be increased by all sectors. The "system" of child care and early education is woefully underfunded, short-changing children at the very ages when investments in them have the greatest impact on them and the largest pay-back for society. Consequently:

✦ Both the federal government and the states must increase their child care and early education commitment to ensure that funds are available to help families leaving welfare for work *and* working poor parents who are trying to remain independent of welfare. States must at least provide the matching funds necessary to draw down the federal money available under the 1996 welfare law. The federal government must give all eligible children access to the comprehensive services of Head Start. In the absence of full federal funding, states should follow the lead of Ohio and Georgia to give all their children access to high-quality early education services like Head Start. Governments at all levels must help early education programs expand their hours to better meet the needs of working parents.

✦ While unpaid parental leave has been a step forward, America's working parents need *paid* parental leave—like that afforded to workers in most other wealthy industrial democracies. A social insurance plan of wage replacement for a modest time for new parents would have positive effects for children, parents, and the nation.

✦ Local governments should expand their role in helping to improve the affordability, quality, and supply of child care and early education services.

✦ The business sector must become a much stronger partner in meeting the child care and early education needs of their low- and moderate-income employees—both by providing more on-site care and by helping parents pay for care. Businesses also should help the larger community address child care quality, supply, and affordability needs.

✦ Community agencies need to see child care and early education as a top priority, making funds, space, resources, and volunteers available to expand and improve families' child care and early education options.

Children need *good-quality* child care and early education. Children need to be safe, stimulated, and well nourished, in care that is developmentally appropriate. Good-quality early childhood programs can make a difference in the lives of children, particularly low-income children. Consequently, all investments in child care and early education, from whatever sector, must:

✦ Support services that keep children safe and nurtured, and that help them develop so they can enter school ready to learn.

✦ Ensure that low-income children have access to comprehensive services—including high-quality education, nutrition, health, and social services—and parents have access to education and support services.

Food and Nutrition

The 1996 welfare law targets food assistance programs that aid low-income families with children for the deepest reductions in their history. Food stamps—the nation's most important child nutrition program—will bear the brunt of these cuts, absorbing more than 50 percent of *all* spending reductions made by the welfare law. The food stamp cuts will total more than $27 billion over the next six years. Two-thirds of these food stamp cuts will be achieved by reducing, denying, or terminating assistance to low-income families with children.

Slightly more than half of all food stamp recipients are children. The welfare bill's food stamp changes will reduce the food purchasing power of every low-income family in the nation that uses food stamp assistance to help feed its children. Poor legal immigrant children will be affected most severely. For most of them, food stamps will be terminated altogether. Even children who are citizens but whose parents are legal immigrants will see their families' food supplies sharply reduced, because only the citizen children, rather than the whole family, will receive food stamp benefits.

The welfare law also makes potentially harmful changes in several other child nutrition programs. It substantially restructures and cuts federal resources for the family day care component of the Child and Adult Care Food Program (CACFP). It also reduces the amount of money that schools, municipal agencies, and nonprofit organizations receive for the meals they serve during the summer months to children in low-income areas through the Summer Food Service Program (SFSP) for children. These cuts are deep enough that a significant number of providers could drop out of the programs. The new welfare law also ends the federal grants to states to help them expand the school breakfast and Summer Food Service programs.

The only positive development in 1996 on the food assistance front is that other proposed cuts and program changes did *not* happen. Threats to block-grant school feeding programs dissipated in late 1995 and early 1996, and congressional proposals to let states convert the food stamp program into a block grant and to make even deeper cuts in food stamp benefits were defeated.

Actions in 1996 unrelated to the welfare law also create serious problems for the Special Supplemental Food Program for Women, Infants, and Children (WIC). WIC is one of the most effective of all federal programs; every $1 spent on WIC food and nutrition counseling for pregnant women is estimated to save $3.50 in medical, income support, and special education costs for low-birthweight babies. WIC funding for Fiscal Year 1997 is inadequate to maintain current WIC participation levels, unless Congress passes a supplemental appropriation.

Some of the harsh effects of these changes can be mitigated. But that will require action on three levels: Congress and the President must enact legislation easing some of the most severe cuts in the welfare bill and providing supplemental funding

This chapter was prepared in cooperation with Robert Greenstein, executive director of the Center for Budget and Policy Priorities. Contact the Center at 820 First St. NE, Suite 510, Washington, DC 20002, 202-408-1080.

for WIC, states must assume some of the responsibilities shed by the federal government (especially for legal immigrants), and nonprofit organizations and food program operators across the country must engage in new and creative efforts.

How the Food Stamp Reductions in the New Welfare Law Affect Children

All food stamp households will face either reduction or termination of their benefits. When fully implemented, the new welfare law will slice total food stamp assistance by almost one-fifth. A substantial portion of the food stamp benefit reductions come in the form of across-the-board benefit cuts for *all* recipients, including families with children, the working poor, the elderly, and people with disabilities. Only about 2 percent of the law's food stamp savings will come from provisions to reduce fraud and abuse, to impose tougher penalties on recipients who violate program requirements, and to reduce administrative costs.

Studies repeatedly have shown that America's food pantries and other emergency food assistance facilities can't meet existing need, much less the increased need this law will create. Studies also have demonstrated the adverse effects on children of even mild forms of undernutrition and of hunger—including iron deficiency anemia (which is associated with impaired cognitive development), fatigue, trouble concentrating in school, and stunted growth.

Two-thirds of the food stamp benefit reductions will affect families with children—including poor working families. In Fiscal Year 1998, the first full year of the cuts, the nearly 7 million families with children receiving food stamps will lose an average of $435 in food stamp benefits. Since the average gross income of a poor family with children in 1995 was $600 a month—just 54 percent of the poverty line—this is a large loss. The 2.3 million food stamp households in which someone is employed, most of which are families with children, will lose an average of $355 in food stamp benefits in 1998. These benefit reductions deepen over time: In 2002, poor working households will lose an average of $465 in food stamp benefits. The government itself says that the minimum short-term diet (the "Thrifty Food Plan") for a family of four now costs $4,800 a year, so this loss will impair families' diets seriously.

Several of the welfare law's food stamp provisions will affect children particularly. Food stamp

◆ Fifty-two percent of food stamp recipients in 1995 were children.

◆ The nearly 7 million families with children receiving food stamps will lose an average of $435 a year in benefits because of the new welfare law's cuts.

◆ More than 15 million children received free or reduced-price lunches in 1996.

legislation that was enacted in 1993 would have remedied a long-standing inequity in the food stamp benefit structure. Elderly and disabled households that receive no government housing assistance and pay more than half of their incomes for housing long have received a larger food stamp benefit, in recognition of the fact that their high housing costs leave them less money to spend on food. Families with children that pay more than half their incomes for housing receive a smaller, less adequate upward adjustment in their food stamp benefits. For some poor families with children that face high housing costs, the food stamp rules count a portion of the money they must use to pay rent as available to purchase food. As a result, their food stamp benefits fall short of what they need to feed their families adequately throughout the month.

Congress designed the 1993 legislation to address this problem, requiring the food stamp program to treat families with children that incur high housing costs the same way it long has treated elderly and disabled people. The change was being phased in, and was scheduled to become fully effective in January 1997. The new welfare law, however, stopped this reform. As a result, many poor families with children that pay very large portions of their incomes for rent and receive no government housing assistance will continue to have trouble simultaneously paying their rent and utility bills and feeding their children.

The new welfare law also freezes *permanently* at $4,650 the limit on the market value of a car that a family may own and still qualify for food stamps. The frozen limit is only 3 percent higher than the limit initially set in 1977. But since then, used car prices have nearly tripled, rising 187 percent. As automobile costs rise with inflation in the years ahead, growing numbers of working poor families that need cars to commute to work, especially working poor families in rural areas and parents needing to get to suburban jobs from inner cities, are likely to become ineligible for food stamps because of this freeze. The legislation also freezes several other parts of the benefit structure that previously kept pace with inflation, most notably the food stamp "standard deduction"—the amount deducted from the income of most food stamp households for the purpose of calculating benefit levels.

Whether Congress will revisit any of these issues in 1997 remains unclear. President Clinton, upon announcing in early August 1996 that he would sign the welfare bill, said the food stamp

CHILDREN AND FOOD STAMPS

The welfare law's biggest cuts came in food stamps. Children make up more than half of all food stamp recipients.

Food stamp recipients by age, Fiscal Year 1995

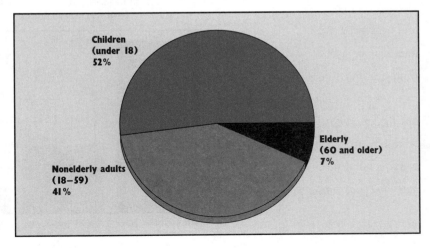

Children (under 18) 52%

Elderly (60 and older) 7%

Nonelderly adults (18–59) 41%

Source: U.S. Department of Agriculture.

cuts were too deep, and singled out the provision relating to poor families with children that face high housing costs as one that ought to be changed.

The Plight of Immigrant Children

Between April 1, 1997, and August 22, 1997, *all* legal immigrants now receiving food stamps will be removed from the food stamp program unless they are refugees or asylees in their first five years in the United States, children whose parents have been employed here for 40 calendar quarters, or children of members or veterans of the U.S. armed forces. The overwhelming majority of poor legal immigrant children now receiving food stamps—about 200,000 children—will lose them. The same rules also will apply to legal immigrants who enter the country in the future.

It is unclear how these children will get adequate nutrition. Moreover, legal immigrant children with disabilities also will lose their Supplemental Security Income (SSI) benefits, and newly arriving legal immigrant children will be ineligible, for at least five years, both for non-emergency

Medicaid and for federally funded cash assistance under the new welfare block grant.

States will be able to make policy choices that can help protect legal immigrant children. Under the new welfare law, states decide whether immigrant children who were legally here before the welfare bill became law can receive aid under the Temporary Assistance for Needy Families (TANF) welfare block grant and also whether these children can continue to qualify for Medicaid. Because the new law will make most of these children ineligible for food stamps, regardless of how poor they are, the welfare block grant may be the only assistance enabling their parents to buy adequate food during times of need.

States also can elect to use their own funds to provide food stamp–type assistance for legal immigrant children who no longer qualify for federal food stamp aid. As of late December 1996, Maryland and Washington State were considering this approach.

The new welfare law also allows but does not require states to terminate the eligibility of *undocumented* immigrant children and pregnant women, and certain small categories of legal immigrant children, for WIC, for CACFP, and for SFSP. The

---

FOOD PROGRAMS FOR CHILDREN

Millions *of poor and near-poor children who benefit from free and reduced-price school lunches are not being served by the school breakfast and summer food programs.*

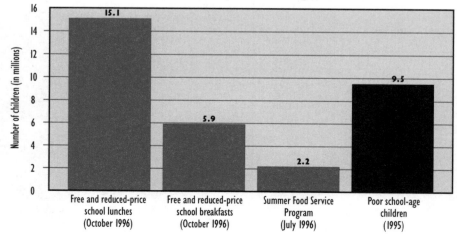

Number of children receiving free and reduced-price school lunches, school breakfasts, and summer meals, and number of poor school-age children

Number of children (in millions)

- Free and reduced-price school lunches (October 1996): 15.1
- Free and reduced-price school breakfasts (October 1996): 5.9
- Summer Food Service Program (July 1996): 2.2
- Poor school-age children (1995): 9.5

Source: Mathematica Policy Research Inc.

child nutrition programs historically have been among the few types of programs for which undocumented immigrant children have been eligible.

As of the end of 1996, no state had acted to bar these children from WIC or the other child nutrition programs. A number of states have realized that doing so would be cumbersome administratively and could cost them significant sums of money over time. For example, if undocumented pregnant women are denied WIC, the incidence of low birthweight among their newborns is likely to increase. Their low-birthweight babies will be U.S. citizens, because they will have been born on U.S. soil, and consequently they will be entitled to Medicaid coverage if they are poor or near-poor. Medicaid coverage for low-birthweight infants is costly, and states bear a share of Medicaid costs. Thus, a state decision to deny WIC to undocumented immigrants—in addition to increasing low-birthweight births, child anemia, and possibly even infant mortality—probably would increase the state's Medicaid costs.

The Child Nutrition Reductions

The federal child nutrition programs —school lunches and breakfasts, WIC, the SFSP, and CACFP—have been an essential bulwark against child hunger and malnutrition for school-age children and for infants and preschoolers. But the new welfare law reduces these child nutrition programs by $2.9 billion.

More than 85 percent of these reductions come in CACFP, which primarily helps pay for meals provided to children in child care centers and family day care homes. Most of these cuts will result from reduced federal support for meals served in family day care homes that are not located in low-income areas or operated by low-income providers.

Until now, the family day care home part of this program has been the only component of any major federal child nutrition program that both is open to children in poor and nonpoor areas alike and also offers the same reimbursement rate for all children, regardless of their family income (although that rate is moderately lower than what

CACFP pays child care *centers* for meals for low-income children). Approximately two-thirds of the CACFP expenditures for family child care have supported meals served to children whose family incomes exceed 185 percent of the poverty line. Many small family day care providers have become licensed so they could get the benefits of CACFP; an attractive feature has been that providers were not required to undertake the paperwork to document children's family incomes.

Under provisions of the new welfare law that take effect on July 1, 1997, existing rules and reimbursement rates will apply to family day care homes that are in low-income areas, or are operated by low-income providers (with "low-income" defined as income below 185 percent of poverty). But for other homes, the law will cut aggregate meal reimbursements about in half, based on the presumption that they serve children who have less need. These homes can opt to have the local CACFP–sponsoring organization that helps them with paperwork administer a means test for children served; where this is done, the homes will continue to receive the current reimbursement rates for meals served to children with family incomes below 185 percent of poverty.

The critical question is whether large numbers of family day care homes that are neither located in low-income areas nor operated by low-income providers will drop out of the program (or, in the case of new homes, not seek to enter it). Their meal reimbursement rates will be reduced substantially, although they still will be considerably higher than those paid to day care centers or schools for meals served to children with incomes above 185 percent of poverty. (For example, child care centers and schools receive 32.5 cents for each lunch they serve to children with family incomes over 185 percent of poverty. Under the new law, homes will receive 95 cents a meal for lunches served to such children.)

Child care experts fear that many homes will drop out of CACFP. If they do, and if others don't try to get into CACFP, the injury to children will be great. In addition to serving as an incentive for providers to become licensed, CACFP is one of the major sources of training and support for family child care providers.

To ensure that many homes do not drop out, states must implement the change carefully. Family day care homes in non-low-income areas are supposed to be allowed to use simple methods to show that some of their children are below 185 percent of poverty, without having to collect income forms from parents. States must explain these rules clearly, long before they take effect, to family day care providers and sponsors. In addition, nonprofit organizations will need to encourage and assist homes to remain in the program, and help them maximize funding with the least administrative burden under the new rules.

Efforts also are needed to bring more family day care homes in low-income areas into the program. States, child care sponsoring organizations, family day care homes, children's advocates, and child care advocates sometimes have been slow to take advantage of federal funds available to help unlicensed family day care homes in low-income areas upgrade their facilities so they can become licensed and take part in CACFP.

In addition to these changes in the family day care home component of the CACFP, child care *centers* also will be affected in one respect by the new welfare law. The law reduces from four to three the number of meals and snacks for which child care centers may receive reimbursement for children in care for more than eight hours a day. This change reinstates a restriction enacted under President Reagan in 1981 and repealed in 1988.

The Summer Food Service Program

The welfare law also cuts, by as much as 20 cents per lunch, reimbursement rates for meals served through the SFSP, which provides lunches and other meals to children in low-income areas during the summer when school food programs are not available and family food budgets are squeezed further as a result. Many child-serving groups, including the Children's Defense Fund's Black Community Crusade for Children, also design full-day recreational and academic programs around these meals, to help keep children in poor communities safe and engaged in positive activities during their out-of-school months.

The effect of the reduced reimbursement rate is not yet clear, but it could prompt some providers to drop out of the program. To encourage providers to continue operating, advocates can note that summer food providers still will receive 16 cents to 17 cents more per lunch than schools and child care centers receive for lunches they serve free to poor children under the school lunch program.

The welfare law also ends the provision of about $5 million a year to states for various initiatives to expand both the SFSP and the school breakfast program, but does not make any significant changes in the school lunch program.

Inadequate Funding for WIC

Despite its proven effectiveness at preventing low birthweight, anemia, and other childhood problems, WIC is funded inadequately for Fiscal Year 1997. At the end of Fiscal Year 1996, WIC was serving 7.4 million women, infants, and children each month. But 1997 funding appears adequate to serve only about 7.2 million monthly. States could have to cut their caseloads by several hundred thousand women, infants, and children in the months ahead.

This has occurred for several reasons. First, Congress appropriated less for WIC for Fiscal Year 1997 than the Clinton Administration requested. Second, prices for several foods provided by WIC have risen faster than expected. Third, both Congress and the Administration were counting on more of the funds appropriated for 1996 to be unspent and to remain available for use in 1997. WIC now faces a funding squeeze, unless Congress and the Administration act swiftly to provide a supplemental appropriation. About $100 million in additional funding will be needed to prevent participation cutbacks.

Opportunities to Help Children

It is essential in 1997 to moderate the damage done in 1996 to nutrition programs for children. Congress and the White House, states, and communities all must act to protect the basic well-being of children and to combat child hunger and malnutrition.

✦ At the federal level, the cuts in food stamp benefits that were made as part of the welfare legislation should be lessened. Families with children that experience very high housing costs should get the same treatment as elderly and disabled households. In addition, poor families with children should not be disadvantaged by the permanent freeze on provisions of the Food Stamp Act that need to keep pace with inflation, such as the limit on the value of a working family's car and the food stamp standard deduction.

✦ The welfare law's severe reductions in food stamps and other assistance for legal immigrants, including legal immigrant children, should be eased.

✦ The federal government should provide sufficient funding in Fiscal Years 1997 and 1998 to prevent WIC cuts and to bring WIC to the bipartisan goal of full funding.

✦ In implementing the welfare law, states should act to ensure that children's nutritional needs are addressed. States also should provide state funds to maintain food assistance for poor legal immigrants.

✦ Communities should work to expand the school breakfast program, and to take maximum advantage of SFSP's potential as a base for creative, community-based summer initiatives that combine food with recreation and academic and cultural enrichment.

Children and Families in Crisis

New research released in 1996 suggests that child abuse and neglect are increasing even more than reports by state child protection agencies previously have indicated. And many of the children identified as abused or neglected are not getting the attention they deserve. Meanwhile, many children are lingering in foster care, and substance abuse by parents continues to add to the strain on the child protection system.

Amid growing caseloads and threats of budget cuts, 1996 was a year of trying to keep heads above water for many services nationwide that work to keep children safe by strengthening families. But there also was new hope in 1996 for children and families in crisis. Public and private agencies, local leaders, foundations, and families continued to engage in the quest to create caring communities that offer family-centered, community-based, comprehensive services to protect children, support families, and help children with serious emotional problems and other special needs. Local efforts were buoyed by such federal initiatives as the Children's Mental Health Services Program and the Family Preservation and Support Services Program, as well as cross-system initiatives in states and foundation-supported activities.

On Capitol Hill in 1996, Congress kept intact the federal guarantee for federal foster care and adoption assistance, as well as other child abuse prevention and treatment programs. But in a sad irony, the new welfare law's elimination of the assurance of basic economic supports for families threatens to create unmanageable new pressures for already-vulnerable families and for the child protection system.

The 1996 welfare law's stated goal is to move families from welfare to work. Clearly, children benefit when their parents find and keep jobs that pay living wages and provide health insurance. But for too many children and families, this goal is not within reach, and in many ways the new welfare law will make it harder, not easier, for parents to support and care for their children and keep their families together.

Child Abuse and Neglect Increase

In 1995, 996,000 children—more than 2,700 a day—were abused or neglected, according to the National Committee to Prevent Child Abuse. This number was up almost 25 percent since 1990, but had decreased slightly since 1994.

These data come from annual counts by the states' child protection agencies of the portion of the 3.1 million children reported abused and neglected whose cases were investigated and confirmed. But a different type of data, released in 1996 by the U.S. Department of Health and Human Services (HHS), suggests that these totals—as disturbing as they are—may greatly understate the extent of child abuse and neglect. The National Incidence Study (NIS) of Child Abuse and Neglect showed that child-serving professionals believed 2.8 million children were abused or neglected in 1993. That was almost triple the number of abused and neglected children reported by public agencies to HHS for that year. The NIS is based on interviews not just with public child protective service staff, but also with professionals in police departments, schools, hospitals, health and mental health agencies, and child care centers.

Particularly troubling was the NIS finding that the number of children seriously injured nearly quadrupled between 1986 and 1993. Yet the number of reports investigated by child protection agencies stayed about the same in each year, decreasing the percentage of children whose abuse or neglect was officially investigated from 44 percent in 1986 to 28 percent in 1993. The volume of abuse and neglect reports, it seems, may have surpassed the ability of public agencies to investigate them. Unfortunately, the NIS did not determine why so many more children's cases were not investigated. Some may never have been reported, or were reported but screened out before being investigated. Regardless, the findings suggest that more work must be done to ensure that children in danger get the attention they deserve, and that children with less serious needs are helped appropriately, not necessarily through the child abuse and neglect system.

According to the NIS data, younger children and girls were more likely than older children and boys to be harmed or at risk of harm. As in earlier versions of the NIS, there were no significant differences found in the incidence of maltreatment by race, but family income did make a very large difference. Children in families with annual incomes below $15,000 per year, for example, were more than 25 times more likely to be seen by the interviewed professionals as abused or neglected than children whose families earned $30,000 or more per year.

Welfare Changes Likely to Put More Children at Risk of Harm

Threats to the protection of children are likely to continue to grow as the new welfare law is implemented and adds to families' financial stress, making it harder for them to support their children. Already-vulnerable families that have parents who lack education or job skills, or are trying to overcome domestic abuse or substance abuse, likely will be most in danger of losing benefits in instances when the work requirements and time limits are applied rigidly. The demands on child protection agencies will increase as families' needs intensify. Desperate families unable to feed or shelter their children may be forced to turn to the child welfare system for help, after living doubled-up or tripled-up with family and friends

- In 1995, abuse or neglect of 996,000 children was investigated and confirmed by child protection agencies.

- The number of children seriously injured by abuse nearly quadrupled between 1986 and 1993, according to interviews with child-serving professionals.

- An estimated 468,000 children were in foster care during a one-day count in 1994—a 16 percent increase since 1990.

- More than 1.4 million children lived with grandparents with no parents present in the household in 1995—up 66 percent since 1989.

- By 1996 estimates, approximately 4 million to 5 million 9- to 17-year-olds have serious emotional disturbances, and fewer than one in four received treatment recently.

and moving from shelter to shelter. But that system's prevention resources are severely limited, and too often out-of-home care will be the only option.

The new welfare law also eliminated the federal Emergency Assistance Program—a critical child welfare safety net in 44 states—and consolidated its funds into the Temporary Assistance for Needy Families block grant. The Emergency Assistance Program previously supported emergency help for families in crisis, including homeless families and victims of domestic violence. Cuts in the Title XX Social Services Block Grant and the Supplemental Security Income (SSI) program for disabled children also will squeeze further already-stretched resources.

Recent experiences of some large urban areas provide a preview of what likely is coming nationally. In Los Angeles County, for example, child abuse and neglect referrals jumped 12 percent immediately following the September 1991 cut of 2.7 percent in California's Aid to Families with Dependent Children (AFDC) grants, and then jumped another 20 percent the following year, when California cut AFDC grants another 5.8 percent.

Foster Care Grows, as Does Care with Kin

One of the few positive outcomes of the 1996 welfare debate, after much hard work by child protection advocates, was preservation of the guarantee that all children in need of foster care or adoption assistance under federal rules will receive it. Congress rejected proposals to block-grant foster care and adoption assistance and other targeted child abuse prevention and treatment initiatives—partly because of concern that the welfare law's deep cuts in cash assistance and other aid could increase demands for such services, resulting in serious human and fiscal costs. In a typical state, placing in foster care even 1 percent of the children formerly on cash assistance would boost the foster care caseload by almost 20 percent—at a per-child cost four to five times that of cash assistance.

The number of children in care already is rising nationally, although declining in some states. An estimated 468,000 children were in foster care as of June 30, 1994 (a 16 percent increase since 1990), according to data released in 1996 by the American Public Welfare Association. While nu-

ABUSE AND NEGLECT TRENDS

Between 1985 and 1995, the number of children reported abused or neglected rose 61 percent, to 3.1 million, while the number of children with investigated and confirmed reports rose 36 percent, to just under 1 million.

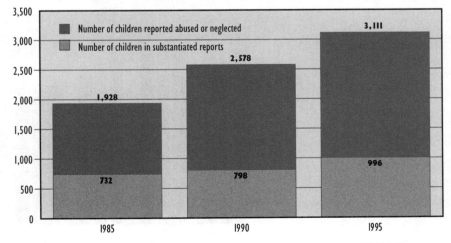

Number of children reported abused or neglected and number of children with substantiated reports, 1985–1995 (in thousands)

Legend:
- Number of children reported abused or neglected
- Number of children in substantiated reports

	1985	1990	1995
Number reported abused or neglected	1,928	2,578	3,111
Number in substantiated reports	732	798	996

Sources: 1985: American Association for Protecting Children, American Humane Association; 1990: U.S. Department of Health and Human Services, National Center on Child Abuse and Neglect; 1995: National Committee to Prevent Child Abuse.

merous factors have contributed to the increase in the need for foster care, three trends affecting current and future caseload sizes were notable in 1996:

✦ Too few children are leaving foster care for permanent homes. Multistate Foster Care Data Archive data from California, Illinois, Michigan, New York, and Texas (which together represent almost half of the children in care nationally) reveal that the number of children entering care continues to exceed the number leaving care, and that discharges have leveled off in recent years, after an increase between 1988 and 1991.

President Clinton in late 1996 took an important step toward seeing that children waiting in foster care can be placed in permanent homes: He instructed HHS to devise a plan early in 1997 to at least double by the year 2002 the number of children in foster care who are adopted or otherwise placed permanently with families. He also ordered other federal departments to promote private-sector involvement in adoptions and increase adoptions by federal employees.

Congress also acted in 1996 to retain the federal Adoption Assistance Program, which contributes a federal share to state payments to assist with the adoption of children with special needs, and enacted a first-ever adoption tax credit, with a larger credit going to parents who adopt special-needs children. Unfortunately, the tax credit's impact on the adoption of children with special needs probably will be minimal, because the credit is not "refundable" (available as a payment to people who owe little or no taxes). Often, the foster parents who seek to adopt special-needs children in their care have incomes too low to benefit from a nonrefundable credit. To reduce the amount of time that children of color wait for adoption, the 1996 Amendments to the Multiethnic Placement Act clarified that race, color, and national origin cannot be used to delay placements of children with foster or adoptive parents. Such laws complement initiatives by the W.K. Kellogg, Dave Thomas, and Annie E. Casey foundations, which seek to increase community involvement in ensuring permanence for children.

✦ Since illicit drug use began rising in the early to mid-1980s, substance abuse by parents has contributed to the increase in child protective services and foster care caseloads. Experts say

AGE OF VICTIMS

The youngest children are most vulnerable to abuse and neglect. Infants and toddlers alone make up nearly 20 percent of abused or neglected children.

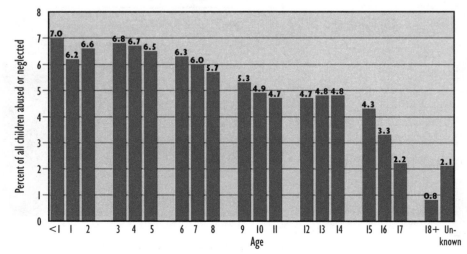

Age of abused and neglected children, as a percentage of all maltreated children, 1994

Source: U.S. Department of Health and Human Services, *Child Maltreatment 1994: Report from the States to the National Center on Child Abuse and Neglect.*

a substantial portion of the children who come to the attention of the child protection system are in families with alcohol or other drug problems. This should not be surprising: A special analysis of the 1991 National Household Survey on Drug Abuse, conducted for HHS, reported that in 1991, parents of almost 20 percent of all American children had used illicit drugs in the preceding year.

Fortunately, new evidence is demonstrating that effective treatment produces a wide range of positive effects. Illicit drug use declined by about 50 percent in the year after treatment among the more than 4,000 clients of programs supported by federal Center for Substance Abuse Treatment grants, according to a 1996 report of the National Treatment Improvement Evaluation Study. There also were significant declines in criminal activity, physical and mental health visits, and homelessness, as well as in fear among families with children of losing child custody due to alcohol or drug problems. Further, there was evidence of improved employment rates. Equally encouraging was a 1995 Center for Substance Abuse Treatment report on the two federal programs that fund residential treatment for women with substance abuse problems and their children. Ninety-five percent of the women who had been pregnant during treatment reported uncomplicated, drug-free births. Seventy-five percent who successfully completed treatment remained drug-free, and substantial numbers obtained employment following treatment, eliminated or reduced their dependence on welfare and, among those referred by the criminal justice system, had no new charges following treatment. Eighty-four percent of the children who participated with their mothers improved their school performance, and two-thirds were returned from foster care. A new analysis for HHS of the California Drug and Alcohol Treatment Assessment reports that the benefits of substance abuse treatment exceed the costs by 6-to-1 for mothers not on welfare, and by 2.5-to-1 for mothers on welfare.

✦ AIDS is killing growing numbers of mothers, leaving their children orphaned. While new advances in AIDS treatment may, over time, create a dramatic shift in the course of the epidemic, AIDS deaths, particularly among women, now leave behind tens of thousands of

IN RELATIVES' CARE

The number of children living with relatives with no parent in the home grew 75 percent in the first half of the 1990s. The number of children living with grandparents with no parent present increased 66 percent during the same period.

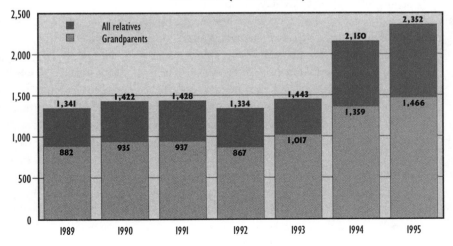

Number of children being raised by relatives with no parents present, 1989–1995 (in thousands)

- All relatives
- Grandparents

Year	All relatives	Grandparents
1989	1,341	882
1990	1,422	935
1991	1,428	937
1992	1,334	867
1993	1,443	1,017
1994	2,150	1,359
1995	2,352	1,466

Source: U.S. Census Bureau, *Current Population Reports*, March 1986–1995.

children. In New York State alone, the annual number of AIDS-related deaths rose tenfold from 1985 to 1994. HIV infection and AIDS now surpass any other single cause of death for mothers of children and youths in New York State. If current trends continue, by the end of the year 2001, an estimated 58,000 New York children and youths (under 21) will have lost their mothers to AIDS since 1981, according to *Families in Crisis*, a 1996 report of the Working Committee on HIV, Children, and Families. Nearly 90 percent of the children will be Black or Hispanic. To help ensure permanent placement and continuity of care for the children, New York and eight other states have adopted "standby" guardian laws. Without complicated court proceedings, a standby guardian is vested with authority for a child when the parent is incapacitated (or dies), but authority reverts to the parent when she or he is well.

As the number of children needing foster care has grown, more grandparents and other relatives have become surrogate parents. The U.S. Census Bureau recently reported that in 1995, 1,466,000 children lived in households headed by a grandparent with no parent present—a 44 percent increase since 1993, and a 66 percent increase since 1989. The Multistate Foster Care Data Archive reports that in 1993, kinship placements constituted about 35 percent of the state foster care caseload in New York, just over 40 percent in California, and more than 50 percent in Illinois. Many relatives do not receive foster care payments, with the proportion varying by state and depending in part on state policies.

Among new approaches in 1996 to addressing the needs of the increasing numbers of relative caregivers, HHS allowed Illinois and Delaware to establish subsidized or supported guardianship demonstration programs, which can assure children of permanent homes when reunification with the parents is not possible and the relatives do not want to adopt. In Illinois, for example, participating relative caregivers are eligible for subsidized guardianship arrangements and payments (partially reimbursed to the state with federal funds) for children who have been in the state's custody

for two years or more, who have been with the caregiver for at least one year, and who have formed a mutual attachment and commitment.

Private initiatives to support the growing number of relative caretakers also are under way. In 1996, the Brookdale Foundation awarded its first grants through its Relatives as Parents Program to 15 community-based agencies and five state offices on aging in the eastern United States. They will receive training, technical assistance, and seed grants to increase services for grandparents and other relatives who have taken on surrogate parenting responsibilities.

Higher Incidence of Children with Serious Emotional Disabilities

New estimates in 1996, prepared by a multidisciplinary group convened by HHS's Center for Mental Health Services, revealed that 9 to 13 percent of 9- to 17-year-olds (approximately 4 million to 5 million children) have serious emotional disturbances that significantly interfere with their functioning at home, in school, or in community activities. The prevalence rate was found to be higher for lower-income children. The group also noted that fewer than one in four children with serious emotional disturbances had received mental health care recently.

Despite these children's need for help, the new welfare law further endangers many of them by limiting their access to SSI—which enables families to care for disabled children at home, and to obtain the special equipment, transportation, or specialized child care that is often necessary. An estimated 250,000 to 315,000 disabled children—many of whom have serious emotional disabilities—could lose SSI eligibility, and an estimated 15 percent of them also will lose Medicaid.

In a more positive development, 1996 brought good news from the communities that are bringing together mental health, health, child welfare, education, and juvenile justice agencies to coordinate services to young people with serious emotional disturbances. Preliminary findings from an evaluation of the 22 initiatives (funded by HHS's Children's Mental Health Services Program, which saw its budget increased by 17 percent in

1996) found that school performance improved for children at all grade levels, and especially for children in the elementary grades.

There was also cause for optimism in the small, but important, steps taken by Congress to begin to end the discrimination in health insurance coverage against children and adults with mental health problems. The Mental Health Parity Act of 1996 requires that the aggregate annual and lifetime benefit limits in a health insurance plan be the same for mental and physical health care, if the plan covers mental health care at all.

New Approaches to Child Protection

The hallmark concept of *community-wide responsibility* for child protection was advanced in 1996 by federal, state, and local initiatives. HHS issued final regulations in 1996 governing the Family Preservation and Support Services Program, which Congress passed in 1993: The regulations emphasize the importance of child and family services being community-based, involving neighborhood organizations and parents in their design and delivery, and being accountable to the community and the clients' needs. As well, the 1996 reauthorization of the Child Abuse Prevention and Treatment Act included a new demonstration grant program to promote innovative partnerships between public child protective service agencies, private agencies, neighborhood-based resource centers and other family support programs, schools, and religious congregations, to ensure appropriate responses to abuse and neglect cases.

Florida and Missouri already are beginning to involve public and private service providers, and sometimes family members, in child protective service agency assessments and responses to reports of child abuse and neglect, while keeping a strong public agency role in investigations of serious abuse. Such efforts respond directly to the NIS recommendation that formal child protective service investigations target the children who most need them.

Under Florida's Family Services Response System, county agencies now can establish partnerships with families and community agencies and organizations, to develop innovative solutions to reported child abuse and neglect. In one county, for example, public health nurses or Healthy Start workers contact the families in which there are reports of abuse or neglect of infants exposed to alcohol and other drugs at birth, and school nurses respond to some of the other reports. In another county, "Community Support Agreements"—involving the child protective service agency, the family, and a friend, relative, teacher, or other community professional who agrees to help the family resolve its problems and monitor the child's safety—are used in lower-risk cases. The state estimates that the Family Service Response System is being used for about 75 percent of the families reported to child protection agencies. At the same time, a number of county child protection agencies have developed new relationships with law enforcement agencies to strengthen their role in the criminal investigation and prosecution of cases involving serious maltreatment.

The Edna McConnell Clark Foundation has awarded grants to communities in both Florida and Missouri, as well as in Iowa and Kentucky, to further develop models for community-based approaches to protecting children.

Another emerging approach promoting community responsibility for child protection is Family Group Decision-Making, mandated in New Zealand and now being used in cities in at least seven U.S. states. Family and community members, sometimes together with staff members of child protection and other child-serving agencies, meet to plan appropriate help for families in which there has been abuse or neglect. The goal is to help the family take responsibility for its children and alter its behavior.

A decision to hold a family group conference is made when it is likely in a particular case to increase child safety and when parents agree to participate. A family group may include extended family, friends, neighbors, clergy, nurses, or other professionals whom the family and child see as helpful. The family group assesses the family's situation and determines how the child can be cared for and kept safe; if the agency staff disagrees with the final plan, the family or juvenile court has the final say. The agency staff then helps the family group provide the needed services and supports. In 1996, the American Humane Association's Children's Services Division and the American Bar Association's Center on Children and the Law published materials to guide communities using family group conferences.

A major goal of the three-year-old Family to Family initiative, supported by the Annie E. Casey Foundation and operating in six states, has been to develop a system of neighborhood-based foster care. Family to Family trains foster parents who live in or near the same communities as the birth parents to work as a team with the birth parents for changes in the home that will allow the child to be returned more promptly or, when that is not possible, to facilitate adoption.

In Cleveland, Ohio, Family to Family has been a catalyst for community involvement in reforming the Cuyahoga County Department of Children and Family Services to protect local children. When the reforms began, the county agency had lost 100 foster parents, and children awaiting foster homes were sleeping every night in the agency's lobby. Four years later, no children sleep in the lobby, the number of foster homes has increased by more than one-third, placements with relatives have increased greatly, the percentage of children placed in institutional care has been cut in half, and adoptions have increased 80 percent. Child protection workers receive some of their initial training in neighborhood centers. Then they are assigned to specific neighborhoods, where they know and build trust with people in the community. Community residents have created their own networks of foster homes and supports for foster parents, since they realized that so many children had been removed from their community by the child protection system; now attempts are made to place children needing out-of-home care within their own school systems and near their parents.

Los Angeles County Reaches Broadly to Provide Protection and Permanence

In 1991, faced with substantial growth in numbers of reports of child abuse and neglect, births of babies exposed to drugs, and out-of-home care caseloads, the Los Angeles County Department of Children and Family Services (DCFS) committed to a multi-pronged approach to:

◆ Protect children from abuse and neglect;

◆ Help families keep their children safe;

◆ When necessary, provide temporary homes that would promote children's growth and development;

◆ Move children to legally permanent homes, with their own families or with adoptive families;

◆ Give youths who reach adulthood in DCFS care an opportunity to succeed; and

◆ Form community partnerships to provide a comprehensive array of services that support and protect families and children.

Since then, important steps have been taken on each front. Although still being refined and expanded, the different activities together provide a picture of what is needed to strengthen families and communities and protect children.

Steps to help families and communities keep children safe got under way first. The Family Preservation Committee, a public–private–community partnership, helped assess the need and build consensus for family preservation services, and helped DCFS create and implement nine Community Family Preservation Service Networks in January 1993. The networks were located in the six communities with the highest rates of poverty, unemployment, and out-of-home placements; together, these communities accounted for about 40 percent of the children in DCFS's care.

A Community Advisory Council and lead agency oversee each network. Targeted families are those whose children are at risk of placement but may remain at home under protective supervision. A Multi-Disciplinary Case Planning Committee in each network—made up of the case-carrying staff from DCFS and from probation, mental health, substance abuse, and other community agencies, helpful individuals, and family members—draws up a service plan in each case and meets regularly to assess the family's progress.

Each network must provide a variety of in-home services, including emergency caretakers and outreach visitors. Each also provides parent training; individual, group, and family counseling; mentoring; mental health treatment; self-help groups; transportation; and flexible funds for family emergencies. Through linkages with other providers, families can receive other services, such as health care, child care, substance abuse treatment, employment training, income maintenance, and housing assistance. Network funding from DCFS is based on the number of children in out-of-home care within the community and the families' levels of need.

Between March 1992 and October 1995, out-of-home placements in the initial six communities increased 1 percent, compared with a 38 percent increase in all other parts of the county. An evaluation for the state Department of Social Services by Walter R. McDonald and Associates reported that DCFS's approach to family preservation has succeeded in focusing on the entire family and helping families better meet their children's needs, has increased agencies' cultural awareness, and has promoted collaboration and involvement by nontraditional community agencies. By September 1996, 24 community family preservation networks had been established, covering two-thirds of the county.

Meanwhile, family support activities to help children before and after they need DCFS protection or get involved with other public agencies—including youth leadership training and mentoring, youth employment readiness, violence prevention, recreation, tutoring, child care, and health promotion—are being conducted by 17 collaboratives, with funding under the federal Family Preservation and Support Services Program.

In 1995, DCFS launched a Community-Based Placement pilot program in one of the family preservation network communities, to increase the placement of children in foster homes within rather than outside their neighborhoods, improve visitation, keep children in their neighborhood schools, and actively involve foster parents and school staff in assessing and treating families' needs, to promote permanent placements. Specially trained foster parents who live in the community serve as parenting role models for the birth parents, let birth parents visit frequently, facilitate

thorough assessments of the children, and help with case planning. In return, they are eligible for a monthly bonus above their regular foster care payments. Schools make their family resource centers available for recruitment and other meetings after school and on weekends. In the first pilot site, the number of available foster homes already has doubled, foster children have remained in their own schools, and school staff members are actively involved in ensuring that foster children get the help they need. The program now is being expanded in the county and throughout the state.

DCFS also has increased its efforts to get children into permanent homes, through either reunification or adoption. Twenty-six percent of children who entered foster care in the state during the first six months of 1988 were still there four years later, according to the Child Welfare Research Center at the University of California, Berkeley. Of the children who entered foster care as infants, almost two out of five had had two placements and a similar proportion had had three or more. DCFS successfully supported legislation to facilitate adoption, and is promoting public education about permanency and specialized training for agency and court staff, attorneys, paid foster and relative caregivers, community family preservation network representatives, and school and health agency personnel. It is also working toward more aggressive advocacy for permanency in the courts.

DCFS also has given special attention to teenagers who are preparing to leave its care. In addition to independent living services funded by the federal Independent Living Program, the department provides:

✦ Transitional housing for up to 18 months for homeless 18- to 20-year-old foster youths and former foster youths who agree to be in school or work and have regular contact with a social worker.

✦ Scholarship assistance to enable every young person aging out of foster care to attend and stay in college or trade school, if other help is not available.

✦ Help from a Jobs Development Section in finding and keeping employment. The section has made significant progress toward its goal of generating 300 full-time and 1,000 part-time jobs from county departments and private industries. In the summer of 1996, 762 jobs were provided by the county alone. Thrifty Payless, Jack in the Box, and Gap Kids are among the businesses that have provided special training and employment options for foster care youths.

(For more information, contact Peter Digre, DCFS director, at 213-351-5602.)

Opportunities to Help Children

It is essential that we ensure that children are safe, in nurturing families and communities. Local, state, federal, and private efforts must be expanded to enhance and enforce parental responsibility, and to broaden community responsibility, accountability, and capacity for protecting children.

In cities, neighborhoods, and towns, businesses, congregations, and community organizations must pool their resources and work with public and private service providers to establish services and supports that address basic economic and social needs of families and children. Such partnerships also should address the special demands caused by substance abuse, domestic violence, homelessness, and the challenges associated with teen parenting and with caring for children with serious emotional problems or other disabilities. Individuals—extended family members, friends, neighbors, and others—also have a central role and responsibility to lend a hand to those nearby who need extra support. Effective services should be implemented together in communities and neighborhoods, so their combined impact can be realized.

There also must be attention to repairing the worst safety-net holes created by the new welfare law. Parents who lack education or job experience, or who have been victimized by substance abuse or domestic violence, should get help early so that they do not fall through those holes. They must not be left without sufficient help to find employment, fall outside the newly narrowed welfare rules, and be forced to take their children to the door of the child protection agency. Trained staff members should assess families' needs as they apply for cash assistance, so job preparation will address problems that otherwise could prevent vulnerable parents from moving into employment. States also must apply the new work requirements and time limits in a way that does not deter grandparents and other relatives who are raising kin from seeking assistance if they need it. Children, including those with disabilities, must be assured of basic income assistance if our nation is to honor its commitment to child protection. Such investments are both humane and fiscally responsible, when contrasted with the long-term costs of out-of-home placements.

States must ensure that they have in place the legal framework, the public and private services, the trained staff, and the public will necessary to keep children safe by supporting families in their childrearing responsibilities, and, when children cannot be cared for safely at home, by finding adoptive or other permanent families. Service providers and courts should attend to the individual needs of children and families, and to the fact that what happens to children when they first enter the child welfare system directly affects their ability to move to permanent families in a timely fashion.

Leadership is needed at the federal level, too. Federal laws and programs should emphasize the primacy of the safety of children, and promote state-level policies and activities that respond definitively to the serious abuse of children. But they also must recognize the need, in the vast majority of cases of child maltreatment, for services and supports that will enable families to take responsibility for their children and protect them, with help from their communities. The federal government also must expand its commitment to prevention, to increased supports in and for communities, and to permanent homes for children who now wait too long for loving families.

Children, Violence, and Crime

In many ways, fear *for* our children's safety was twisted into fear *of* our children in 1996. Truths about violence and youths were obscured by politicians' and media hyperbole portraying today's young children as a coming wave of "superpredator" youths. In fact:

◆ After a big increase, violence committed *by* youths has decreased recently for the first time in a decade. While no amount of brutality by or against young people can be tolerated, honest examinations of demographics, crime trends, and the potential of prevention efforts do *not* indicate that today's young children should be objects of fear tomorrow.

◆ Children and youths are 10 times more likely to be victims *of* violence than to be arrested *for* violence.

◆ Crimes committed with ever-more-available guns account almost entirely for the terrible surge of violent crime by youths that the nation experienced from 1987 through 1994.

◆ The most punitive of the currently popular responses to youth crime—such as "three-strikes-and-you're-out" laws that would count an act of juvenile delinquency as a strike, and laws that would put children in adult courts and adult prisons—are less cost-effective than common-sense prevention, individualized justice, and graduated sanctions.

The best news for violence prevention in 1996 was found in communities that showed they can do much to reclaim safety for children. Although Congress pulled back from funding prevention efforts in 1996, in many areas communities took steps to protect children by creating safe havens after school, on weekends, and in the summer; participating in community policing; and developing programs that work with courts to hold juvenile offenders accountable and help rehabilitate them. And although Congress was a reluctant participant in 1996, incremental gun control laws continued to gain momentum at the federal and state levels, and stepped-up enforcement of existing gun laws by police and communities has begun to make a difference and to slow the illegal firearm trade that is robbing too many of our children of their childhoods and even their lives.

Children as Victims of Violence and Gunfire

More than 1.6 million 12- to 17-year-olds reported that they had been the victims of violent crime (other than murder) in 1994 (the most recent year for which data are available by age). That total, as bad as it is, does not include another very pervasive form of violence against children—abuse at the hands of their own parents or caretakers (see the Children and Families in Crisis chapter). Most children who suffer violence, whether in their homes or communities, are victims of adults. Four of five juveniles murdered in 1994 were killed by adults, and a majority of *all* violent victimization of 12- to 17-year-olds is committed by adults.

For a decade, guns drove an appalling rise in child deaths. The number of children who died each year because of gunfire nearly doubled between 1983 and 1993. In 1993, the year for which the most recent complete data are available, 5,751 children under 20 died from gunfire—one child every hour and a half, or the equivalent of a classroomful of children every two days. Although more than half the children who died from gunfire that year were White, Black male 15- to 19-year-olds suffered the greatest proportionate toll. Young Black males are now five times as likely as their White male counterparts to be victims of gunfire.

Nearly two-thirds of the child gun deaths were homicides. The number of children murdered by guns tripled between 1984 and 1994, while the number of children who were victims of non-gun homicides remained flat. After homicide, the largest cause of youth gun deaths is suicide. Guns are used in two out of three youth suicides, and are far more likely than other methods of suicide attempts to cause death. Black male youth suicide rates have skyrocketed, driven by a 300 percent increase in gun suicides between 1980 and 1992. Accidental shootings present another danger to children: Gun accidents killed 526 children in 1993, more than one child each day.

Juvenile Offenders

For nearly a decade, beginning in the mid-1980s, juvenile violent crime—and public concern about it—mounted steadily and rapidly. Between 1985 and 1994, juvenile arrests for violent crime (murder, forcible rape, robbery, and aggravated assault) rose 75 percent. But juvenile arrests for violent crimes were *down* 2.9 percent in 1995—the first drop in a decade. Most encouragingly, arrests of youths for homicide fell dramatically in both 1994 and 1995, down 22.8 percent since 1993. And the earliest reports for 1996 indicate another big drop in homicides in general in big cities and, likely, in homicides by juveniles.

A combination of factors is believed to have contributed to these reductions in youth violence, including increased partnerships between schools, community groups, parents, and law enforcement agencies; stepped-up efforts to keep adults from providing guns to children illegally; improvements in medical technology and experience that may keep alive more children with serious gun injuries; and other societal changes, such as a subsiding of the crack trade and a major drop in all crime and homicide in most big cities (New York City had fewer homicides in 1996 than in any year since 1968).

At the same time that efforts to reduce youth violence are beginning to bear fruit, some commentators—focusing on particularly heinous but isolated crimes by a few youths, and on population

+ In 1994, 2,661 children under 18 were homicide victims and 1.6 million 12- to 17-year-olds reported that they had been victims of other violent crimes.

+ In 1993, 5,751 children under 20 were killed by gunfire. That's nearly twice the number of child gun deaths recorded 10 years earlier.

+ After a decade of large increases in juvenile violence, juvenile arrests for violent crime have fallen: Violent crime arrests declined 2.9 percent between 1994 and 1995, and juvenile homicide arrests fell 22.8 percent between 1993 and 1995.

+ Of every 20 youths who are arrested, 19 are arrested for nonviolent crimes.

projections for the future—proclaimed a "coming wave of superpredators" or "a teenage time bomb." But no teenage population boom is coming: In 2010, the percentage of juveniles, relative to the total population, will be 7 percent—the same as it is now and has been every year since 1989, and lower than the level before 1989.

The recent increase in violent crimes by youths has been concentrated among a very few children, primarily in severely stressed communities. Less than one-half of 1 percent—one in 200—of all 10- to 17-year-olds were arrested for violent offenses in 1994. Of all youths arrested, 19 of 20 are arrested for nonviolent crimes. And about one-third of all juvenile homicide arrests occur in just four cities: Los Angeles, Chicago, Detroit, and New York. Nationwide, 80 percent of counties had no juvenile homicides in 1994, and another 10 percent had one.

In fact, the real wave that has swept away so many of our children, as both victims and perpetrators, has been the tidal wave of guns into communities. *Gun* crime is virtually the only type of youth crime that has risen over the past decade. While juvenile arrests for homicides with guns have quadrupled, juvenile arrests for homicides *without* guns haven't risen at all since 1984. And

other weapons-related offenses have risen as steeply as homicides. By contrast, property crimes, by far the most common offenses committed by juveniles (outnumbering violent crimes 5-to-1), have remained flat over the decade. What we have been witnessing, then, has been not a drastic overall change in youth crime, but essentially a very sharp and very serious increase in crime with guns. Because juveniles have increasingly easy access to guns, what formerly would have been a fist fight or knife fight, or a serious act of delinquency, now too often involves a gun and is far more likely to result in death or a homicide arrest.

Violence Prevention Efforts *Can* Reduce Violent Crime

With youth population rates flat and youth violent crime rates apparently beginning to fall, the opportunity is ripe to increase investments in proven prevention strategies for teenagers and young children, so they can become nonviolent youths who achieve success in their families, schools, friendships, and activities.

Research and evaluations of community programs are proving that parental and community

THE NATURE OF JUVENILE CRIME

The juvenile arrest rate for property crime—the major category of juvenile crime—has remained relatively constant over time, and has been at least five times the violent crime arrest rate for the past two decades. But the rates of weapons offenses and violent crimes have climbed dramatically during this time.

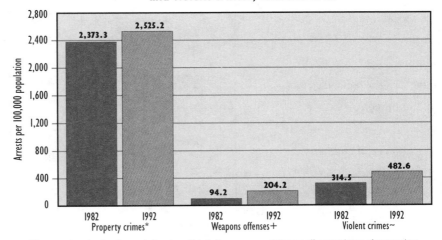

Juvenile arrest rates for property crimes, weapons offenses, and violent crimes, 1982 and 1992

*Property crimes: burglary, larceny-theft, motor vehicle theft, arson.
~Violent crimes: murder, forcible rape, robbery, and aggravated assault.
+Weapons offenses: violations of weapons laws.
Note: All arrests are classified by the most serious offense involved.

Source: National Center for Juvenile Justice.

action can do a great deal to keep children safe—that children who are kept busy with positive activities and watched over by caring adults have better odds of staying out of trouble and out of harm's way, and becoming successful adults, than children without those opportunities. Such actions not only reduce violence, but can reduce drug and alcohol abuse, school dropout, and early sexual activity, as well.

Two new studies confirm the value of prevention in reducing violence and crime. *Making a Difference*, released in late 1995 by Public/Private Ventures, showed that children who had Big Brothers or Big Sisters were less likely to abuse drugs or alcohol, have trouble in school, or hit another person. They also experienced improved relationships with their families and peers. Key to the success of the mentoring relationship was the program's screening, training, and supervision of the adult volunteers, suggesting the importance of structure and support for volunteer efforts.

A second study, released in 1996 by the RAND Corporation, emphasized that it is far more cost-effective to work with delinquent youths, to hold them accountable and rehabilitate them, than to take such punitive approaches as "three-strikes-and-you're-out" laws. Three intervention programs—offering training to parents struggling with delinquent youths, providing such youths with financial incentives to graduate from high school, and monitoring and supervising high-school-age youths who have begun to be delinquent—eliminated greater numbers of serious crimes per dollar spent than did three-strikes incarceration. Graduation incentives, for example, averted 250 serious crimes per $1 million spent, compared with just 50 crimes averted by three-strikes laws.

Congress recognized the importance and value of investing in community-based prevention in the 1994 crime law, which set aside more than $500 million a year in a Violent Crime Trust Fund, fully paid for by reductions in spending on the federal government work force. Congress sought a balanced approach to crime fighting that supported police, prisons, *and* prevention. Among the community-based initiatives were three—Community Schools, Ounce of Prevention, and Family and Community Endeavor Schools (FACES)—to fund schools and community groups to operate after-school, summer, and other programs to prevent crime and violence and promote academic and social achievement.

GUNS AND HOMICIDE

J *uvenile arrests for gun homicides quadrupled between 1984 and 1994. At the same time, arrests of juveniles for homicides that did not involve guns remained stable. Similarly, the number of children murdered with guns tripled from 1984 to 1994; non-gun murders of children rose very slightly.*

Juvenile arrests for firearm and non-firearm homicides

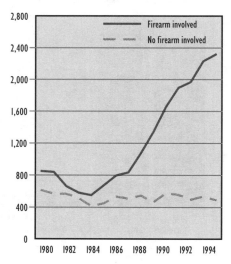

Homicides of juveniles, with and without guns

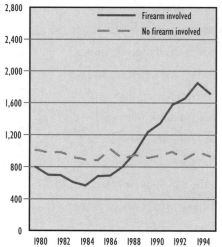

Source: National Center for Juvenile Justice.

But in 1995 and 1996, the White House failed to press for such funding and Congress upset the balance in the 1994 law by removing most of the prevention money and adding it to the police funds through a newly created Local Law Enforcement Block Grant. At the same time, Congress made it harder for communities to spend any of that block grant money on youth crime prevention programs. As a result, community prevention programs are severely underfunded (see chart, page 66).

Graduated Sanctions Reduce Crime and Rehabilitate Youths

While an investment in prevention does pay dividends for the majority of children, even well-funded programs in every community would not eliminate all juvenile crime. Increasingly, evaluations of local programs indicate that the best way to hold accountable and try to rehabilitate the children arrested for delinquent offenses is to respond to each and every offense with prompt sanctions and services that match the seriousness of the offense and the particular youth's previous record—in other words, individual consideration and graduated sanctions.

The Fulton County Truancy Intervention Project in Georgia, for example, responds to truancy—often a warning sign for more serious delinquency—with a specially trained judge and a volunteer lawyer, a faster court timetable, prioritized referrals to resources and agencies, and sufficient probation services. Between 1992 and 1995, only 11 of the 450 youths who had been truant were back in court while on probation.

More seriously delinquent youths can be referred to programs like the Wayne County Intensive Probation Program in Michigan. The youths live in their homes throughout the nearly yearlong treatment period; have at least daily meetings and telephone contacts with their caseworkers to monitor school attendance and behavior; and receive individual, group, and family counseling, educational planning, and job training and placement services. An evaluation showed that these home-based programs were just as effective in controlling crime as incarceration, but at one-third the cost—an estimated saving of $8.8 million over three years.

For the most violent offenders, who must be kept in secure care to protect the community, places like the Florida Environmental Institute (nicknamed the "Last Chance Ranch") offer solu-

SUICIDE, GUNS, AND BLACK MALE YOUTHS

Gun suicide rates for Black male youths rose sharply in the late 1980s (just as Black male youth homicides began to climb). At the beginning of the 1990s, the overall suicide rate for Black male youths —driven by this increase in gun suicides—for the first time surpassed the suicide rate for all youths.

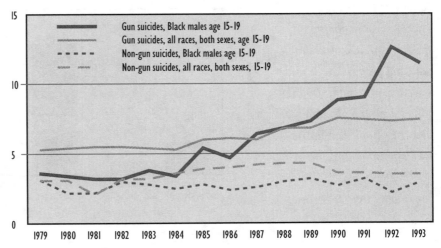

Gun and non-gun suicides among all 15- to 19-year-olds and among Black male 15- to 19-year-olds, per 100,000, 1979–1993

Gun suicides, Black males age 15-19
Gun suicides, all races, both sexes, age 15-19
Non-gun suicides, Black males age 15-19
Non-gun suicides, all races, both sexes, 15-19

Source: National Center for Health Statistics.

tions. The Ranch, which houses 40 youths in an isolated area of the Everglades and has a high staff-to-youth ratio, runs an 18-month program based on a philosophy of education and hard work, a system of rewards and sanctions, positive relationships with staff role models, and a strong aftercare component. After youths return to their communities, they hear from staff at least four times a week and must adhere to a strict curfew. If they break curfew or commit another offense, they are returned to the Ranch. One-third of Ranch graduates were convicted of violent crimes in the three years after leaving, compared with two-thirds of those leaving traditional incarceration facilities.

Many of the solutions recently embraced by states and by some members of Congress ignore such individualized justice and graduated sanctions, and cling to outdated, discredited notions based on punishing children as adults. Rep. Bill McCollum introduced the Violent Youth Predator Act in 1996, proposing to put children as young as 13 in adult courts and adult jails. A number of senators proposed lowering the federal death penalty age from 18 to 16. And the federal Office of Juvenile Justice and Delinquency Prevention in the U.S. Department of Justice, established in part to prevent children from being put in adult jails,

issued rules in 1996 relaxing national standards that protect children from being jailed with adults, or jailed for such non-criminal behavior as skipping school or running away.

But disagreement within and between the political parties in Congress left broader issues unresolved in 1996, and the core law on juvenile justice, the Juvenile Justice and Delinquency Prevention Act (JJDPA), was not reauthorized. One more year of funds for JJDPA was provided—$170 million, $26 million more than in Fiscal Year 1996. Included was $16.5 million for graduated sanctions and more than $49 million for prevention. The debate about the long-term future of the JJDPA will continue in 1997.

In other 1996 legislation, Congress took one major step away from protecting children in prison. The Prisoner Litigation Reform Act (PLRA) dramatically limits prisoners, including juveniles, from seeking relief in the courts from the physical or sexual abuse they may experience while in jails or prisons, by prison staff or other prisoners.

Meanwhile, states continued to embrace the idea of transferring youths to adult courts and prisons. In Florida, which has transferred more youths to adult court than the rest of the states combined, a 1996 study found that youths who had been tried

SKIMPING ON PREVENTION

*C*ongress recognized the effectiveness of community programs that keep children safe and prevent crime and violence, and authorized significant funding from a special trust fund. But the actual appropriations for 1995, 1996, and 1997 were far smaller than the trust fund allowed.

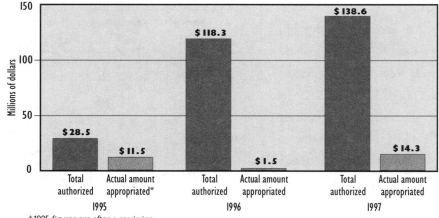

Federal 1994 crime bill allocations to, and actual appropriations for, selected youth crime prevention programs, Fiscal Years 1995–1997, in millions of dollars

*1995 figures are after a rescission.
Notes: Programs included are Family and Community Endeavor Schools (Department of Education), Community Schools (Department of Health and Human Services), and Ounce of Prevention (Department of Justice). Total authorized is the amount Congress made available for the program when creating it. Actual amount appropriated is the amount the sitting Congress approved to be spent on the program that year.
Source: Calculations by Children's Defense Fund.

in adult court went on to commit crime again more often than comparable youths handled by juvenile courts. Also, more than half the time, moving groups of children to adult courts automatically sweeps up nonviolent offenders, who most often can be rehabilitated by the combination of sanctions and services offered by the juvenile courts. What's more, moving children into adult facilities, whether they are tried in adult or juvenile court, far too often leads to serious physical and sexual abuse: Children in adult institutions are five times more likely to be sexually assaulted, twice as likely to be beaten by staff, and 50 percent more likely to be attacked with weapons, compared with children in juvenile facilities.

Regulating Guns Reduces Violent Crime

Gun control initiatives to keep children safe and alive received growing and unanticipated support in 1996.

Communities worked with police in innovative ways to stop illegal guns from being provided to children, with recent enforcement action buoyed by two surveys. One study in Boston found that children with illegal guns usually have newer, trendier guns, which are easier to track back to dealers than the older guns more common with older criminals; another, by the federal Bureau of Alcohol, Tobacco, and Firearms (ATF), showed that only 1 percent of the 160,000 licensed gun dealers nationwide are responsible for 51 percent of all illegal gun sales. ATF, through its gun-tracking program, worked with local police in several cities nationwide to identify and arrest gun dealers and middlemen responsible for illegal gun sales, including sales to children and criminals.

Meanwhile, between March 1, 1994, and June 30, 1996, the 1993 Brady law stopped handgun purchases by 102,822 felons, fugitives, and others who are not permitted to buy guns. Eighty-five felons a day have been stopped from buying firearms. Despite this success, the Brady law's requirement that local officials participate in background checks has been challenged by some sheriffs as an unconstitutional burden imposed on states by the federal government. The Supreme Court heard

this case argued in late 1996, and will announce its decision in 1997. If this part of the Brady law is overturned, Congress could enact new legislation in slightly different form to continue the law's progress, as it did in 1996 when it effectively overrode the Supreme Court's 1995 invalidation of gun-free zones around schools.

Overall, the 104th Congress yielded a positive, if limited, record on gun control. First, the ban on personal ownership of assault weapons was *not* repealed, although the House voted in early 1996 to repeal it. A second, positive development was passage of a ban on firearm ownership or purchase by anyone convicted of a domestic violence misdemeanor involving a spouse, partner, or child. (The Brady law bars only felony offenders from having guns.) Finally, members of Congress supported by the National Rifle Association (NRA) tried but failed to cut the Centers for Disease Control and Prevention's $2.6 million funding for scientific research on firearm injuries.

In the states, struggles over laws allowing most citizens to carry concealed weapons continued, as the crime-reducing value of these laws remained in great doubt. Six states moved in 1996 to allow more guns to be carried concealed, but seven states rejected such measures.

Pursuing another strategy, in late 1996 Massachusetts Attorney General Scott Harshbarger proposed regulating guns as a consumer product, requiring trigger locks and minimum quality standards so that guns, like household products, meet safety standards covering malfunctions and accidents, particularly those involving children. While final regulations still are pending, this new approach holds the promise of reducing the number of gun accidents and the number of cheap, poorly made guns in circulation and, therefore, available to children. Other localities, most notably 21 jurisdictions in California, have banned these "junk guns" outright.

Boston Pulls Together to Save Children

Not one child was murdered with a gun in 1996 in Boston; one young child, tragically, was beaten to death by an adult relative. Although one death is still too many, that's a big improvement, compared with the 16 child homicides Boston faced in the peak year of 1993. What is Boston doing right? And how can other cities do the same?

Deborah Prothrow-Stith, M.D., assistant dean at Harvard's School of Public Health, reports that Boston's efforts to prevent violence began in 1982, when the Boston Violence Prevention Project developed a training module in violence prevention. Over the years, hundreds of city residents received this training, and learned broader violence prevention concepts to adapt to their communities. Many of those trained then launched prevention initiatives that, in turn, affected thousands of Boston-area youths—initiatives that included youth organizations like Teens Against Gang Violence; summer opportunities at the Boys & Girls Clubs and at basketball camps; and congregation-based programs like the Ten-Point Coalition, where congregants mentor delinquent youths and assist their families.

By the 1990s, the mayor's office began to provide significant support for violence prevention, funding streetworkers, community centers, and a Safe Neighborhoods micro-grants fund. The city also aggressively pursued federal funds for violence prevention, including money from the U.S. Departments of Justice, Education, and Health and

Television Violence

In 1996, concern continued to grow not only about the violence children live with in their families and communities, but also about the effects on children of the huge amounts of violence they see on television. Most children spend as much time, if not more, with television as in school or with family members. Children watch an average of three to four hours of television a day, and over the course of these hours *each year* they see 1,000 murders, rapes, and aggravated assaults. Ironically, violence is particularly prevalent in children's programs: In 1992, children's shows featured 32 acts of violence an hour. Moreover, a 1996 study by the cable industry and the University of California at Santa Barbara found not only that most television shows contain violence, but that the violence usually has no consequences, such as harm, pain, or punishment.

In response to parents' increasing concern about children and television violence, Congress passed "V-chip" legislation as part of the Telecommunications Act of 1996. The V-chip (short for violence chip) will be included in new television sets beginning in 1998, to enable parents to program their televisions to block categories of shows, based on their ratings.

At the end of 1996, the Implementing Group formed by the television industry announced a rating system with age-based categories (Y, Y7, G, PG, PG-14, M) similar to those used for rating movies. This system bitterly disappointed parents' and children's groups, which unanimously had advocated for a content-based system that would include ratings such as V, S, and L, to indicate the presence and the level of violent, sexual, or adult-language content. Four out of five parents surveyed by the National PTA, and 75 percent polled by Roper, preferred a content-based system to an age-based system that fails to tell parents, for example, whether a show is rated PG because of violence or language. Parents' groups and child advocates are urging a prompt and fair review of parents' satisfaction with the new system, and will encourage individual broadcasters and cablecasters to follow the lead of HBO (Home Box Office, a cable channel), which provides content ratings that give parents the information they need to guide their children's television viewing.

Human Services. Some of this training and funding was targeted to communities hardest hit by violence, such as Roxbury and Dorchester. But the violence prevention movement rippled throughout the Boston area, as a broad range of professions and communities made violence prevention a priority and participated in coalitions cutting across these lines.

Leadership in law enforcement also was critical. According to Jim Jordan, director of Strategic Planning and Resource Development for the Boston Police Department, community policing restored accountability to a mistrusted police force and led to improved relationships between police officers, probation officers, and social service workers and the community. Working with other agencies, police have been able to identify at-risk youths and respond to a neighborhood's particular needs, whether it be to break up a drug trade, monitor youths on probation, or provide more youth activities. In addition, ATF, on the heels of the 1993 Brady law, provided federal support in interrupting the supply of illegal guns to Boston. Local grassroots leadership on gun control provided critical political support for these efforts.

Ultimately, all of these individual efforts have come together and grown to have a big impact on Boston's children and the safety of their communities: 16 children were murdered in 1993, six in 1994, four in 1995, and one in 1996. But as youth worker Ulric Johnson of the Adolescent Wellness Program emphasizes, the roots of violence—poverty, discrimination, hopelessness, and family breakdown—must be attacked to truly reduce all forms of violence against children, now and in the future.

Still, the steep decline in youth homicides indicates that violence prevention has taken hold in Boston, involving coalitions, broad public education, investments in prevention, new laws, and new strategies for enforcing old laws. But it all started with just a few people, committing to saving children from more violence. And, in the end, that's the central lesson to be learned from the Boston experience. As Prothrow-Stith says, "Just get started."

(For more information or help in getting started, contact the mayor's Office of Health and Human Services, Director, Juanita Wade, 617-635-3446.)

Opportunities to Help Children

The construction of a new, safer world for our children will depend in great part upon the work of communities that provide children with positive alternatives to the lures of the streets; open their schools, houses of worship, and recreation centers for tutoring, activities, and counseling after school, on weekends, and in the summer; work with police to remove illegal guns; and organize religious and community groups to mentor parents and youths in need of support and guidance. But also needed are state, local, and national policy initiatives to make children safer from violence, to motivate children to stay out of trouble, and to hold juvenile offenders accountable.

✦ Congress should fulfill its commitment to the crime and violence prevention funding provisions in the 1994 crime law, which set funding for the three programs listed in the chart on page 66 at $171 million in 1998, $212.5 million in 1999, and $220.5 million in 2000—still short of what is needed, but 10 times what was approved in the most recent Congress. Programs like Community Schools, which allow communities to create safe havens for children after school and in the summers, must be fully funded and reinvigorated. Congress, states, and school boards should find additional ways to open schools early and keep them open late and on weekends, with schools or community groups providing care and programs for children.

✦ States and the federal government need to take the weapons that are killing children away from children and from adults who would harm children. One important way to do this would be to ban junk guns (also known as Saturday night specials), which have no sporting purpose because of their poor quality and small size. These guns have been banned from importation since 1968, but a domestic market sprang up and boomed in the 1980s, and these cheap, easy-to-conceal guns fed much of the recent rise in gun homicides, gun suicides, and crime. A ban would require domestic companies to follow the same quality standards that foreign companies have followed since 1968. Other efforts could focus on making guns less dangerous to children (by adding trigger locks, for example), and on state or federal one-gun-a-month limits on firearm purchases. After Virginia passed such a law, the number of guns seized by police in the Northeast and traced to Virginia gun dealers dropped dramatically.

✦ The renewed debate on JJDPA reauthorization must focus more on standards protecting children and on investments in crime prevention and strong juvenile court sanctions. Also needed are efforts to give juvenile courts the resources and alternatives with which to respond to almost every juvenile offender—from the truant to the murderer—with appropriate sanctions and services. Drug courts and other alternatives that respond to the vast majority of offenders (19 of 20) who are not violent need more attention.

Education

At a time when a high school diploma typically is the bare minimum requirement for even a low-wage job, and promising jobs demand college degrees, most of our schools are failing to prepare far too many students for success in higher education or the world of work.

By some measures, U.S. schools have improved considerably over the past three decades. For much of that time, the achievement gap between White and minority students narrowed. And overall, we are graduating more young people from high school and sending more to college than ever before. However, the diplomas and degrees awarded to our students too often mean too little. Fundamentally, we are failing to provide most young Americans with the level of skills and knowledge they need if they are to find secure places in the work force and contribute to our national well-being.

Data released in 1996 show that U.S. students' math scores lag behind those of competitor nations, that progress in increasing the number of young people who graduate from high school has stopped, and that 20 years of progress in closing the academic gap that separates low-income students and students of color from others has ended. The gap once again is growing. Further, only one in four of our young people is getting the college education increasingly necessary for his or her economic security and that of our nation.

The primary reasons for low overall academic achievement and attainment, as well as for the renewed growth of the achievement gap, are clear: Too many schools are not providing students with the well-trained teachers, challenging curricula, basic resources, and high standards that students need in order to succeed. And while most schools could do better by their students, schools serving Hispanic, Black, and low-income students tend to have the fewest well-qualified teachers, the most watered-down curricula, the fewest basic resources, and the lowest standards for student performance. Put simply, the students who have the fewest resources outside of school receive the least at school.

Americans must mount a campaign on two fronts to improve the education of our children: We must raise academic achievement for all students, and we must accelerate the performance of schools serving low-income and minority students so that the achievement gap is closed once and for all. Winning the campaign for high-quality education for all students will provide the nation with the human capital we need to keep the U.S. economy vibrant and competitive, and with a citizenry equipped to participate fully and responsibly in the democratic process. For many Americans, a good education offers the surest route out of poverty and a weapon against the effects of racism. And for every child, more and better education converts into greater employ-

This chapter was prepared in cooperation with Amy Wilkins and Kati Haycock of the Education Trust. The Washington, D.C.–based Education Trust works to improve student achievement in kindergarten through college, especially among minority and poor students. For more information, call 202-293-1217, or write to the Trust at 1725 K St. NW, Suite 200, Washington, DC 20006.

ability, more personal income, more options in life, and less dependence.

Schools' Performance

Education matters today more than ever. High-level skills and knowledge are increasingly necessary for success in this high-technology age. Today's college graduate can expect to earn twice the wages of a high school graduate, and nearly triple the wages of a high school dropout—differences that are much larger than in earlier generations.

Report after report, commission after commission has explored and explained the need for high-level universal education. All of these reports and commissions have attempted to prod parents, teachers, principals, school boards, states, and the federal government to take action to improve the quality of education offered in public schools. Many have established education goals for schools. The most visible of these are the National Education Goals.

In 1990, recognizing the national need for a well-educated and highly skilled work force, the nation's governors (including then–Gov. Clinton) and former President Bush established this set of modest education goals for the country to meet by the year 2000. A majority of the goals are indicators of core academic performance and inputs, for kindergarten through college. According to the 1996 report of the National Education Goals Panel, which presented trend data on 11 of the 23 core academic goals, the nation has made slim progress on four goals, no progress on five, and has lost ground on two.

All of the progress has been made in the area of mathematics. Between 1990 and 1992, the percentages of fourth- and eighth-graders meeting the Goals Panel mathematics performance standards increased. But for eighth-graders, this improvement only meant that the percentage meeting the mathematics performance standard increased from 15 percent in 1990 to 21 percent in 1992—leaving 79 percent of all eighth-graders still below the mathematics standard. At this rate of improvement, not until 2018—nearly two decades later than the year 2000 target—will all eighth-graders meet the Goals Panel math standard.

The other two areas of progress reported by the Goals Panel in 1996, again in the area of mathematics, were both in higher education: an increase in mathematics and science degrees awarded, as a percentage of all undergraduate de-

✦ Eighty-six percent of young people have received high school diplomas or the equivalent by age 24. One in seven has not.

✦ Public schools serving few poor children in 1990 spent an average of $6,565 a year per child. Schools in which at least one-quarter of students are poor spent an average of $5,173.

✦ Only one in four young Americans completes a college education.

✦ College graduates now earn twice the wages of high school graduates, and nearly triple the wages of high school dropouts.

grees, and an increase in the number of math and science degrees awarded to women.

Although students have made progress in mathematics, the *Third International Mathematics and Science Study* (TIMSS), published in November 1996 by the National Science Foundation, found that math scores of U.S. students are below the average of the 41 countries participating in the study. Countries significantly out-performing the United States included Korea, Japan, the Czech Republic, Slovenia, and the Russian Federation. TIMSS further found the performance of U.S. students wanting in science. Although U.S. science performance levels were slightly above the international average, our students still performed at lower levels than those in Singapore, the Czech Republic, Japan, Korea, and Hungary.

Math and science are not the only areas in which U.S. student performance falters. Although more literate than students in many other countries, U.S. children still are not reading as well as they should. While most students have mastered basic reading mechanics by high school graduation, far too few have mastered more complex but equally important reading skills. In 1994, 100 percent of 17-year-olds could "carry out simple discrete reading tasks," but only 41 percent could "find, understand, and explain relatively complicated information," according to the Governing Board of the National Assessment of Educational Progress (NAEP). NAEP also found that only one in three U.S. 9-year-olds was a proficient reader.

In too many areas, the nation has made no progress toward the National Education Goals in the past decade—a fact as discouraging as the low performance levels themselves. The November 1996 Goals Panel report found, for example, that:

✦ Between 1992 and 1994, the percentage of fourth- and eighth-graders meeting the reading standards remained unchanged at 30 percent, leaving seven in 10 students performing below the national goal. The news was worse for high school seniors: Between 1992 and 1994, the percentage of seniors meeting their reading standards actually *declined*, from 40 percent to 36 percent.

✦ Between 1990 and 1995, we made no progress in increasing the number of young people completing high school.

Only 86 percent of all students earn high school diplomas or the equivalent by age 24. This leaves one in seven American young people without a high school diploma, which is the bare mini-

INCOME AND THE COLLEGE PREP TRACK

High school seniors who are more affluent are more than twice as likely as lower-income students to be enrolled in a college prep course sequence.

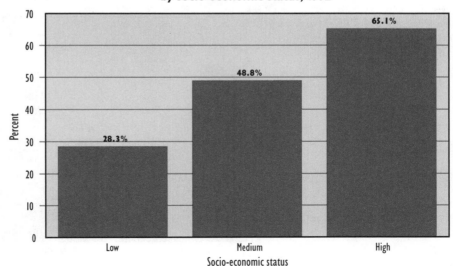

Percentage of high school seniors enrolled in college preparatory track, by socio-economic status, 1992

Low: 28.3%
Medium: 48.8%
High: 65.1%

Socio-economic status

Source: U.S. Department of Education, *A Profile of the American High School Senior in 1992.*

mum demanded by most employers. By 1994, 30 states and the District of Columbia had not reached the year 2000 goal of a 90 percent high school graduation rate.

Another problem is that just 62 percent of all high school graduates enter two- or four-year colleges, and fewer than half of those who enter go on to earn four-year degrees. Ultimately, only one in four of our young people is getting a college education, leaving three-quarters of our young adults inadequately prepared to participate fully in our increasingly complex and competitive economy, and to contribute to U.S. leadership in the world.

The Education Gap

The picture for Black and Hispanic students, and for students living in poverty, is considerably bleaker than the nation's overall educational outlook. Nearly 20 years of progress in narrowing the academic achievement gap that separates low-income and minority students from others has stopped.

Between 1970 and 1988, Black, Hispanic, and Native American students—and the schools that serve them—made striking progress. In just 18 years, the academic achievement gap between Black and White students narrowed by half, while the gap between Hispanic and White students narrowed by one-third. But beginning somewhere between 1988 and 1990, progress stopped. Since then, depending upon grade level and subject, the gap has either remained the same or grown. NAEP data provide painful evidence:

✦ The gap between the math scores of White and Hispanic 9-year-olds *grew* by almost one-third between 1990 and 1994.

✦ By 1994, gaps in reading scores between 17-year-old non-Hispanic Whites and Hispanics, and in science scores between 13-year-old Whites and Blacks, had opened further than their already-unacceptable sizes.

Further, there has been little progress in ensuring that students of color enter and succeed in institutions of higher education.

✦ According to the National Education Goals Panel, the college-completion gap between Whites and Hispanics grew from 15 percentage points to 21 percentage points between 1992 and 1995.

✦ While 58 percent of all White adults have completed some college, only 40 percent of

DROPOUT RATES

Family income greatly affects youths' likelihood of dropping out of high school, whether they are White, Black, or Hispanic.

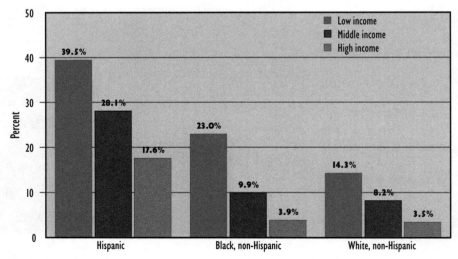

Dropout rates among 16- to 24-year-olds, by income and race/ethnicity, 1994

- Low income
- Middle income
- High income

Hispanic: 39.5%, 28.1%, 17.6%
Black, non-Hispanic: 23.0%, 9.9%, 3.9%
White, non-Hispanic: 14.3%, 8.2%, 3.5%

Source: U.S. Department of Education, National Center for Educational Statistics.

Blacks and only 30 percent of Hispanics have done so.

✦ Twenty-four percent of White adults hold bachelor's degrees, compared with only 13 percent of Blacks and 9 percent of Hispanics.

The public—and many educators—point to non-school problems such as poverty, struggling families, violent neighborhoods, and drug abuse to explain the lagging performance of poor and minority children and the growth of the gap. These conditions matter a lot, but good schools can do much to help children transcend them. Schools in some of the most desperate neighborhoods in America are succeeding every day, proving that poor and minority children can achieve at the highest levels, if they are taught at the highest levels. They are no less able to learn than White and more affluent students, just as U.S. students are no less able to learn than are students in other nations. The difference is in the amount, quality, and targeting of investments that cities, states, and the nation make.

While no single factor can account for the renewed growth of the academic achievement gap, shortages of attention, resources, and expectations explain a great deal of it. During the 1960s, 1970s,

and into the mid-1980s, there was a focused public demand for greater equity in education. A national commitment was made to ensure that students of color and low-income students had access to quality education. This commitment was exemplified by the creation and growth of such programs as Head Start and Title I Compensatory Education. Although discrimination and resource gaps persisted, the marshaling of public commitment and resources began to work, and the number of low-income students and students of color who mastered basic skills increased.

In the past decade, however, before the gap was near being closed fully, the public and policy makers, perhaps heartened by the earlier results, began to focus on other issues. Public attention—and resources—shifted away from inner-city schools. This shift in public attention coincided with two other developments: the emergence of the information economy, demanding not basic skills but high-level skills; and the explosion of such problems as crack cocaine, gun violence, higher poverty levels, and AIDS in many communities. These new crises took up large chunks of local budgets—for law enforcement, for example—and competed with education for public dollars and attention. While the public was looking

INCOME AND EDUCATION

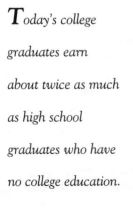

Today's college graduates earn about twice as much as high school graduates who have no college education.

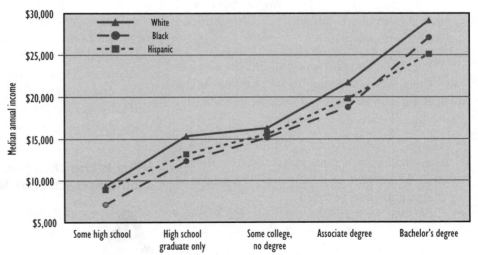

Median annual income by educational attainment, by race and Hispanic origin, 1995

Note: Persons of Hispanic origin may be of any race.
Source: U.S. Census Bureau.

the other way, the achievement bar got higher but the obstacles to learning faced by children in these communities got steeper. And finally, at about this same time, many school districts, seeing a growth in student population, began to relax their standards for teacher hiring and introduced large numbers of under-prepared teachers, mostly into politically weak communities.

Today, the resource gaps between affluent and poor schools, and between White and minority schools, are staggering. The nation has constructed an educational system so full of inequities that often it exacerbates rather than mitigates the problems poor and minority children face. Persistent segregation, tracking of students, lower spending levels, and fewer educational resources—such as well-educated teachers, up-to-date textbooks, challenging curricula, and computers—all combine to reduce the achievement of poor and minority children.

✦ In 1990, America's schools spent an average of $6,565 per child yearly in schools with very few poor children—27 percent more than the $5,173 per student spent in schools in which more than one-quarter of students were poor. The differences between schools with low and high percentages of minority students were smaller, but still significant.

✦ At schools in which more than three in 10 students were poor, 59 percent of teachers reported that they lacked sufficient books and other reading resources. Only 16 percent of teachers in more affluent schools identified such shortages.

Poor, Black, and Hispanic children are also less likely than White students to be enrolled in the college preparatory track or the rigorous math and science classes needed to prepare for life:

✦ While 50 percent of all White students are enrolled in the college prep course sequence, only 43 percent of Blacks and 35 percent of Hispanics are so enrolled.

✦ Only one in four students from low-income families is placed in the college prep sequence.

✦ Only 35 percent of Black and Native American high school students, compared with 53 percent of White students, complete Algebra II and Geometry.

✦ While 26 percent of White high school graduates have completed Physics, only 18 percent of Black graduates and just 13 percent of Hispanic graduates have done so.

While some might believe that low-income and minority students are not enrolled in the more rigorous classes because they are unable to do the work, data from one large California school district tell a different and even more troubling story about race, ethnicity, and student placement. Researchers reviewed the relationship between performance on the Comprehensive Test of Basic Skills (CTBS) and placement in Algebra classes. The study found that 100 percent of the Asian Americans and 87.5 percent of the Whites scoring in the top quartile (one-fourth) on the CTBS were placed in Algebra, but only 51 percent of the Blacks and 42 percent of the Hispanics scoring at the same level were placed in Algebra. Moreover, Asian Americans scoring in the third quartile were more likely to be placed in Algebra than Blacks scoring in the *top* quartile.

Finally, schools serving low-income students too often have lower standards and expectations for students than do schools serving others. A 1994 U.S. Department of Education study compared the English grades and standardized test scores of students in high- and low-poverty schools. The study found that students receiving failing grades at low-poverty schools scored about the same on standardized tests as children receiving B's in high-poverty schools. The same pattern held true when math scores and grades were compared.

In short, we get what we expect from our students, and we expect far too little from low-income and minority students, who are just as capable of doing the work if given good schools and teachers.

Why Is the U.S. Education System Doing So Little for So Many Children?

A careful look at what America is putting *into* its schools explains much about why the quality of education schools are putting *out* is unsatisfactory.

America lags well behind other countries in the area of teacher preparation. According to the 1996 report of the National Commission on Teaching and America's Future, "by standards of...teacher education in other countries, U.S. teacher education has been historically thin, uneven, and poorly financed." The commission pointed out that states pay more attention to the qualifications of veterinarians treating the nation's cats and dogs than to those of the teachers educating our children and youths. More than 12 percent of all newly hired teachers start with no training at all, and another 14 percent start without having fully met state standards. By this calculation, more than one in four U.S. teachers enter the field ill-prepared to meet the enormous responsibilities of teaching our children. And we are losing ground in the area of teacher preparation. The 1996 National Education Goals Panel Report found that the number of teachers holding undergraduate or graduate degrees in the field they teach decreased between 1991 and 1994, from 66 percent to 63 percent.

In addition to pre-service education, ongoing professional development plays a critical role in ensuring a highly effective teaching force. While new teachers in Japan and Germany undergo long-term, structured apprenticeship programs, new teachers in this country have no such opportunities.

As inadequate as teacher preparation is across-the-board, minority students (who are concentrated in schools serving mostly low-income students) and students from poor families are even less likely than other students to have well-qualified teachers:

✦ Central-city high school students have only about a 50 percent chance of having a qualified math or science teacher.

✦ Well under half of the teachers in predominantly minority schools hold bachelor's degrees in the subjects that they teach.

✦ In high-poverty schools, four in 10 of the math classes and three in 10 of the English classes are taught by teachers who do not hold even minors in their subject.

For the most part, we also fail to provide our children with the kind of challenging curriculum that will prepare them to enter and succeed in higher education or to meet the challenges of the workplace. Analysis of student performance on standardized assessments shows that a rigorous curriculum improves scores for all students, yet by 1992, fewer than half of all high-school graduates were completing the full complement of courses recommended in 1983 by the National Commission on Excellence in Education. While this is a vast improvement over the 13 percent who were enrolled in college prep sequences in 1983, it still leaves more than half of our young people unprepared for either the workplace or higher education.

Even when American students are enrolled in courses labeled "high level" or "college prep," the content of those courses too often fails to measure up to world-class standards. According to the TIMSS report:

✦ The content of eighth-grade math classes in the United States is comparable to seventh-grade math in Germany and Japan.

✦ U.S. mathematics classes require students to engage in less high-level mathematical thought than classes in Germany and Japan.

Far too few students are enrolled in the mathematics classes they need. Only 50 percent of all students complete Algebra II and Geometry—the math classes that provide the skills and knowledge expected of entry-level workers by an increasing number of industries. The auto company, Saturn, for example, requires that all assembly-line apprentices demonstrate a mastery of Algebra II and Geometry concepts.

Responses from States and Communities

In response to growing public concern about quality and equity in elementary and secondary education, local and state governments, as well as non-governmental organizations, have undertaken a broad range of actions collectively referred to as "education reform." These efforts have included creation of charter schools, voucher programs, teacher training initiatives, and standards development and implementation.

Some have been heroic efforts to raise student achievement and close the achievement gap, while others have been irrelevant and potentially harmful. However, very few communities and no states have implemented the comprehensive, system-wide reform strategies needed to ensure higher achievement for all students and elimination of the achievement gap.

The charter school concept is receiving a great deal of attention from the media and policy makers. There are fewer than 500 charter schools across the country, compared with 85,000 regular public schools, and there is the risk that the charter school experiments will distract public attention from action needed to improve teaching and learning in all schools. High standards, well-trained teachers, adequate resources, and a challenging curriculum are needed to provide better educations for all students. Education reform efforts that fail to address these issues, as most charter and voucher plans do, never will improve student achievement, even for the very small number of children who participate in them. Proven strategies, such as standards implementation and teacher training, would improve teaching and learning in schools serving the majority of children.

Communities must come together to push for the genuine transformation of all of their schools, even though that work is very difficult and can take a very long time. One community, El Paso, Texas, by working across the entire school system through the El Paso Collaborative for Academic Excellence, increased the number of ninth-graders taking and passing Algebra I by 77 percent—2,599 students—between the 1992–1993 and 1995–1996 school years. Over the same period, the number of tenth-graders taking and passing Geometry increased by 37 percent. In the 1992–1993 school year, Texas classified 15 El Paso schools as "low-performing schools," and only two as "recognized or exemplary schools." By the 1995–1996 school year, El Paso had no low-performing schools and 93 area elementary schools had achieved recognized or exemplary status. El Paso made these gains by focusing the attention of the entire community on a few time-tested strategies: All area schools now require at least three years of math and science for graduation; community-supported standards have been developed for all key academic areas, and teachers are being trained to use the standards in their classrooms; and there has been a relentless focus on in-service teacher training, as well as a comprehensive review and improvement of math and science courses offered to candidates for teaching degrees at the University of Texas at El Paso.

At the state level, small steps are being taken to improve teaching and learning. In most cases, the work is much too slow and the steps are far too small. While 31 states have established standards, only 25 have tied assessments to the standards in all academic areas. Only 17 states reward schools and school districts for making progress toward their standards, and 27 have policies of invoking penalties for failure to make progress. In January 1997, *Education Week's 1997 Quality Counts* report on the quality of U.S. education gave grades of C+ or better to only eight states for the quality of their elementary and secondary teachers. No state received an A. Three states—New Jersey, West Virginia, and New York—received A's for the adequacy of educational resources; 16 states received C or worse, including Arkansas, the only state to receive a failing grade in this area.

The Federal Response in 1996

In the 104th Congress, advocates for better quality and greater equity in education beat back a number of serious policy threats, and also were also able to win significant increases in funding for several key education programs. When Congress shut down the federal government in late 1995 and early 1996, one of the sticking points with the President was education funding. Bolstered by public opinion polls showing the importance to voters of education support, the President fought cuts and sought increases in education appropriations. Eventually, in the midst of a very tough budget climate, the Title I program of assistance to local school districts for compensatory education for low-income elementary and secondary students got a 7 percent increase, from $6.7 billion in Fiscal Year 1996 to $7.2 billion in Fiscal Year 1997. Bilingual and immigrant education, Pell grants, and teacher training got significant increases. The Goals 2000 program, which was meant to provide federal support for state efforts to improve education, got a big boost, from $350 million to $491 million, but Congress greatly watered down federal standards and rules in the program, effectively making it more like a block grant.

Other important congressional developments were:

◆ The defeat of the Gallegly Amendment to the immigration bill. Had this amendment been included, hundreds of thousands of children of undocumented aliens would have been barred from public schools. A broad bipartisan coalition of senators and members of the House recognized that this would do little, if anything, to deter illegal immigration, but would, in the long term, leave millions of America's residents with few skills and little ability to participate in the mainstream society.

◆ The derailment of legislation that threatened a generation of hard-won progress toward equity in employment and education by eliminating the requirement that states receiving federal funds adhere to affirmative action policies in hiring and admissions. Opposed by women's groups, civil rights organizations, education groups, and others, the bill never was brought out of committee for floor action.

Opportunities to Help Children

The pattern of inadequacy and inequity that is so pervasive in our schools is not inevitable. High academic achievement and attainment for *all* U.S. students are absolutely reasonable—and necessary—goals, whose achievement is dependent on national will and commitment to a handful of common-sense steps. The nation must:

◆ Set high, clear, and public standards for all students. Standards should cover all key academic subject areas. Parents and the community at large, not just those working in schools, must know and be invested in the standards.

◆ Ensure that the standards are uniform. The same high standards should apply to *all* schools and *all* students.

◆ Invest equitably and adequately in all schools, including those serving poor and minority children.

◆ Enroll all students in rigorous academic programs, not just students who are thought to be "college material." Watered-down, second-tier classes must be eliminated.

◆ Ensure that all teachers have strong knowledge in their subject areas. Teacher preparation at colleges and universities must improve, and entry requirements for teachers should be toughened and applied. Ongoing in-service professional development must be made a priority.

◆ Hold schools accountable for student progress toward the standards. Progress must be recognized and rewarded, and support must be provided to schools that need help. Consequences must be invoked when schools refuse or fail to make progress.

◆ Monitor progress—or lack of it—continuously. Parents, advocates, and states all must be vigilant, informed, and actively involved in the state of children's education.

◆ Help students meet the standards. Students needing after-school or summer programs, mentoring, or other extra supports must be given all the help they need.

◆ Ease students' entry into and graduation from college. Student aid for low- and moderate-income students must be increased. Funds must not be diverted by schemes that do much for affluent families but too little for those struggling the most with the costs of higher education.

Finally, parents are their children's first teachers, and are responsible for encouraging and helping their children to learn, reading to and with them, and monitoring homework. Parents also need to be involved in their children's schools—to volunteer, to attend school meetings, and to know how well their children are being taught, and, when necessary, to insist that teachers and administrators do better. Parents also need to exercise their responsibilities as citizens by advocating for education with school boards and other local, state, and national elected officials whose decisions affect education quality and equity.

Adolescent Pregnancy Prevention and Youth Development

A number of the circumstances of teens' lives have been improving in recent years. Teen birth rates and youth homicide rates (see Children, Violence, and Crime chapter) have been declining, after years of increases. While providing renewed hope that concerted action by families, communities, and governments at all levels can make a real difference in children's lives, 1996's good news should not cause complacency. U.S. teen pregnancy rates remain extremely high; the share of teen births that are out-of-wedlock continues to rise; and teen drug use continues to grow.

Positive youth development efforts, including educational, recreational, social, and employment opportunities, are essential to teens. They give teenagers the opportunities and motivation to develop to their full potential, and to avoid pregnancy, violence, drugs, and other risks too common among youths. But in 1996, despite a declining teen birth rate and evidence that non-marital births for girls and adult women are more common in states with lower welfare benefits, Congress and the President enacted a welfare law that blamed out-of-wedlock births and teen births on welfare. They took away most financial supports from teenage mothers, they cut off many welfare recipients from family planning supports, and they ignored real investments in youth development and teen pregnancy prevention.

The real answers to teen pregnancy and other youth problems—fixing the bleak environments and conditions that rob too many teens of hope and opportunity—remained largely unaddressed, as did the need to build programs to foster positive youth development. Tackling poverty, lack of health care, poor schools, and domestic and community violence is essential to continuing and accelerating the recent teenage birth rate declines and to improving other indicators of youth well-being. It is especially important now, because the consequences of teen births and antisocial or self-destructive behaviors by teens are so much more serious than in earlier eras. Changing economic circumstances mean there are fewer family-supporting jobs for teen parents and young adults who leave school before entering or completing college, lower lifelong earnings for teen mothers, and higher poverty rates for their children.

A Reversal: Adolescent Childbearing Declines

The birth rate among adolescents has decreased slowly but steadily for four years, regaining some of the ground lost when the teenage birth rate rose by nearly one-quarter from 1986 to 1991. The rate for 15- to 19-year-olds has dropped from 62.1 births per 1,000 girls in 1991 to 58.9 in 1994; preliminary data indicate a further decline, to 56.9 births per 1,000 girls for

This chapter was prepared in cooperation with Susan N. Wilson, executive coordinator of the Network for Family Life Education at Rutgers University. The Network supports the teaching of comprehensive family life education in schools and agencies. Contact the Network at Rutgers University, Livingston Campus, New Brunswick, NJ 08903, 908-445-7929.

1995. The rate of adolescent childbearing decreased in 46 states from 1991 to 1994, according to Child Trends.

The modest but steady progress is very welcome. The teen birth rate in this country had fallen for decades (contrary to popular belief), dropping from 89.1 births per 1,000 15- to 19-year-old girls in 1960 to 50.2 per 1,000 in 1986. But the disturbing and sharp increase from 1986 to 1991 wiped out nearly one-third of the earlier gains.

There is no certain explanation for this decade's renewed improvements. The trend is particularly heartening, however, because the proportion of adolescents reporting that they engage in sexual intercourse has stopped growing, and among those having sex, an increasing proportion report that they use contraception. As many as two-thirds of sexually active adolescents use condoms, although not all the time. Comprehensive youth development programs that inspire teens to work toward productive futures, as well as programs that provide teens with information about abstinence, contraception, and sexually transmitted diseases, are contributing. Experts in the field are encouraged that the decrease in the teenage birth rate

over the past four years has been achieved even while the adolescent abortion rate has been falling.

Both the long-term and the short-term declines in the teen birth rate are more impressive in light of two trends: The age at which teenagers reach physical sexual maturity has been going down, and the age when people marry has been going up. American youths, on average, now reach sexual maturity during the six months following their twelfth birthdays, and are marrying at age 24, three to four years later than they did during the 1950s.

Although the age of first intercourse is dropping—four of five American young people have sexual intercourse before age 20, and the average age of first intercourse is 16 for boys and 17 for girls, about the same as in most northern European countries—the overwhelming majority of teen births still occur among 18- and 19-year-olds. In 1994, 59.9 percent of teen births were to these older teens, 37.6 percent to 15- to 17-year-olds, and 2.5 percent to girls younger than 15.

Despite the resumption of the teen birth rate decline, the number of teen births in this country remains a very deep concern—518,389 babies were born to teen mothers in 1994. While the

✦ The teen birth rate in 1994 was 58.9 births for every 1,000 15- to 19-year-old girls. In that year, 518,389 babies were born to teen mothers.

✦ Only one in four teens giving birth in 1994 was married.

✦ The unemployment rate for 16- to 19-year-olds fell to 16.7 percent in 1996, from 17.3 percent in 1995. But for 20- to 24-year-olds, the unemployment rate rose slightly, to 9.2 percent in 1996.

✦ In 1995, recent illicit use of drugs by 12- to 17-year-olds rose to 10.9 percent, up from 8.2 percent the previous year.

birth *rate* went down between 1993 and 1994, the *number* of births to adolescent mothers increased by 2 percent, because there were more teens. The U.S. teen birth rate remains many times that in most western European countries, and research indicates important reasons why: U.S. teens have less access to sexuality education and to health services, and they experience more societal ambivalence about sexuality and more child and family poverty.

Also discouraging is the long-term trend, which continued in 1994, of a rising number of teen births being to unmarried girls. In 1960, 89 of every 1,000 15- to 19-year-old girls gave birth, but about five out of six of the mothers were married. Of 1,000 girls in 1994, far fewer (59) gave birth, but only one out of four mothers was married. Out-of-wedlock births keep growing as a share of the shrinking teen birth rate.

A complex mix of cultural and economic factors has pushed up unwed parenthood among both teens and young adults in this country and in other countries as well. The incidence of motherhood outside of marriage among *all* age groups has grown in the United States (from 14.2 percent in 1975 to 32.6 percent in 1994), as well as in Canada, in parts of Europe, and elsewhere in the developed world. The high rates of unintended pregnancies and births in this country (60 percent of all U.S. pregnancies in 1990 were mistimed or unwanted, according to the National Academy of Sciences' Institute of Medicine) also cross generational lines.

The birth rate for unmarried Black teens, however, declined in 1994, for the third year in a row, to 100.9 births per 1,000 girls. Indeed, nearly all of the decrease in the teen birth rate from 1993 to 1994 was among Black adolescents. The rate among White teens remained unchanged, and the rate for Hispanic teenagers rose slightly. Still, birth rates for Black and Hispanic teenagers are 2.0 and 2.1 times the rate for White teens, respectively.

Why Is Adolescent Pregnancy a Problem?

Approximately 1 million American teenage girls get pregnant each year; about one in three has an abortion, one in seven miscarries, and slightly over half give birth. Low-income teenagers and those with limited academic skills and successes are far more likely to get pregnant. More affluent teenage girls, and those who are more successful academically and have

SEXUAL ACTIVITY

More than half of teenagers become sexually active by age 18. The average age of first intercourse is 16 for boys and 17 for girls.

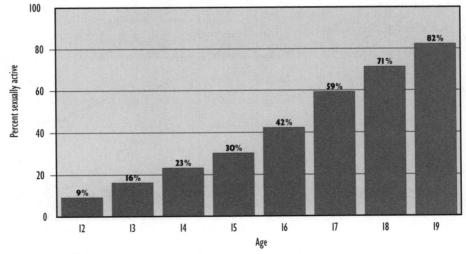

Percentage of teenagers who have had intercourse, by age, 1994

Source: National Commission of Adolescent Sexual Health, Sexuality Information and Education Council of the United States (SIECUS).

higher aspirations, are less likely to get pregnant (and, if they do become pregnant, are more likely to have abortions).

One-fourth of teenage mothers are married and another third are in fairly stable relationships in the first few years of their babies' lives, but many teenage mothers find it hard to attain stability. Whether in stable relationships or not, many find it hard to support their children, because they earn wages below the poverty level and receive inadequate financial support from their babies' fathers.

Children born to teenage mothers have poorer prospects, largely because of the influence of poverty in their lives. They are more likely to be born after their mothers have had little or no prenatal care, to be born prematurely and at low birthweight, to suffer poor health, to grow up without fathers, to live in less supportive homes, to suffer abuse and neglect, to become runaways, to spend time in foster care, to perform less well academically, to become teenage parents themselves, to have less productive work lives, and to serve time in prison.

These are huge prices paid by teen parents and their children, and over time they reduce the nation's productivity. Some of the social costs attributed to teen births really are costs of poverty and failing schools, and likely would be incurred if the same mothers waited until their twenties to give birth, but were still poorly educated, unmarried, or not well connected to the work force. But some significant costs of teen pregnancy are being borne by the public treasury. The 1996 report, *Kids Having Kids: A Robin Hood Foundation Special Report on the Costs of Adolescent Childbearing*, which made special attempts to screen out other factors, estimated the annual public costs of adolescent childbearing to be $6.9 billion, in welfare payments and food stamps, increased medical costs, lost tax revenues, correctional costs, and additional foster care expenses. The report pegged the annual cost of adolescent childbearing plus the costs of other disadvantages faced by adolescent mothers at $13 billion to $19 billion.

Reducing these costs requires reducing poverty and improving low basic academic skills, two underlying causes of many youth development problems—violence, poor health, crime, and drug abuse, as well as teen pregnancy. Kristin Luker of the University of California, author of the 1996 book *Dubious Conceptions: The Politics of Teenage Pregnancy*, says, "The evidence shows there are two

BIRTHS TO TEENS

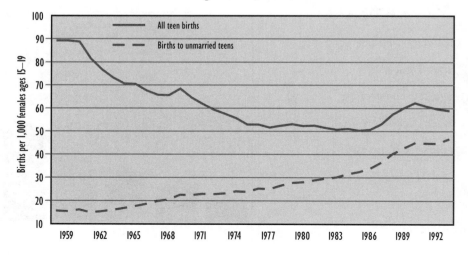

While the overall teen birth rate has declined by a third from 1960 to 1994, births to unmarried girls account for a growing share of this shrinking rate. In 1994, only one of four teens giving birth was married, compared with five of six in 1960.

Trends in birth rates for teens and for unmarried teens, ages 15–19, 1959–1994

All teen births

Births to unmarried teens

Births per 1,000 females ages 15–19

Source: National Center for Health Statistics.

predictors of teen pregnancy: disadvantage and discouragement." In 1994, the Children's Defense Fund and the Center for Labor Market Studies at Northeastern University analyzed government data to show the close links between teen childbearing and poverty and weak basic academic skills, two of the most obvious impediments to hope and opportunity. Indeed, while the Black teen birth rate is twice the White rate, all of that difference (as well as roughly 70 percent of the difference in out-of-wedlock teen childbearing rates) is attributable to the greater poverty and lower basic academic skills among young Black mothers.

Exploitation by Older Male Sexual Partners

The role of significantly older men in teen pregnancy has attracted greater media and public attention in the past few years. A 1993 study showed that more than 70 percent of the babies born to 11- to 18-year-old girls in California were fathered by men four to seven years older than the mothers. Early teenage sex is often non-consensual. In a 1989 study, Luker and others found that 60 percent of girls who had sex before

age 15 said they had been coerced; among girls who had sex before age 14, 74 percent had been coerced.

The negotiation of sexual behavior between sexual partners often is not conducted on even terms—certainly when it occurs between older men and teenage girls, but even among same-age partners. Males are expected to press for sex; females are seen as responsible for contraception, but "nice" girls are not supposed to be prepared to prevent pregnancy. The typical adolescent girl simply is not sufficiently empowered to negotiate sex and contraception with a male partner four or more years older than she is. More research is needed to expose and counter these patterns, removing some of the blame from maligned teenage girls, and focusing more on the responsibility of adult male partners who often are coercive.

The National Campaign to Prevent Teen Pregnancy

Organized in early 1996, in part as an outgrowth of a series of White House meetings on teen pregnancy, the National Campaign to Prevent Teen Pregnancy is a nonprofit, nonpartisan, privately supported effort

YOUNG MEN'S WAGE LOSSES

Young men's weekly wages have plummeted since 1979. Older men's have fallen far less. As fewer young men earn family-supporting wages, fewer marry.

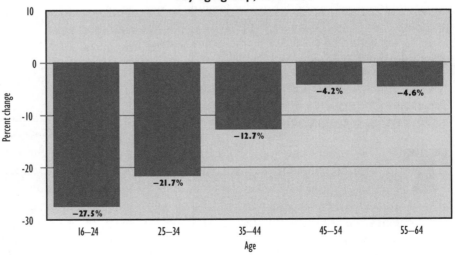

Change in median weekly earnings of full-time male workers, by age group, 1979–1996

- 16–24: −27.5%
- 25–34: −21.7%
- 35–44: −12.7%
- 45–54: −4.2%
- 55–64: −4.6%

Source: U.S. Bureau of Labor Statistics. Calculations by Children's Defense Fund.

dedicated to preventing teen pregnancy by enlisting the media, supporting state and local actions to reduce teen pregnancy, and spreading the word about effective prevention programs. It also seeks to foster a national discussion about how religion, culture, and public values influence teen pregnancy and our responses to it. The Campaign's stated goal is to reduce the teenage pregnancy rate by one-third by 2005.

The Campaign announced plans in 1996 to study a range of likely causes of the high U.S. teen pregnancy rates, including reduced social stigma of teenage pregnancy and non-marital motherhood; few negative consequences for male partners; absence of a clear, forceful message that parenthood is for adults; mass media glorification of sex; the influence of childhood sexual abuse; sexual exploitation by older men; failure of parents to communicate with their children; earlier onset of puberty; the lack of motivation to postpone parenthood; the lack of accessible family planning services; and insufficient information about sexuality and contraception provided to children and adolescents.

The Campaign is examining different types of prevention programs that recognize the ties between poverty, school failure, family problems, and teen pregnancy. The range of programs includes those that emphasize sexuality and contraception education and services; comprehensive youth development programs with little emphasis on sexuality and contraception; early intervention programs, such as Head Start, for at-risk families; and programs that may reduce teen pregnancy while focusing on reducing HIV/AIDS and other sexually transmitted diseases.

Teenage Pregnancy Provisions in the 1996 Welfare Legislation

The 1996 welfare law may well complicate the task of reducing teenage pregnancy. The new federal law makes benefits available to unmarried parents under 18 only if they go to school and live at home, although most school-age mothers already live with their parents (58 percent) or their husbands (12 percent). (Another 12 percent live with other adults, including their adult sexual partners.)

During the welfare debate, 76 prominent economists and social scientists who examined the relationship between welfare and out-of-wedlock childbearing issued a joint statement stressing that there is no significant correlation between births to unmarried girls and women and the amount of welfare benefits provided by various states. But Congress acted on the assumption that welfare increased out-of-wedlock births in numerous ways. Beginning in 1998, the law creates a $50 million abstinence-only education program, with federal specifications of what states will teach: that abstinence is the expected standard for all school-aged children and the only certain way to avoid out-of-wedlock pregnancy and sexually transmitted diseases; and that, for women of all ages, bearing children outside of marriage is likely to cause harm to the child, the child's parents, and society. Although most Americans would agree that these are reasonable messages to give to teens, the approach does nothing to protect teens who already are and will remain sexually active, or those who become sexually active despite the cautions. Such topics as contraception and responsible behavior among sexually active teens are not among those that Congress has authorized.

The welfare law also includes bonuses of added federal funds to the five states that achieve the biggest reductions in their rates of out-of-wedlock births for all age groups (while decreasing abortions) for Fiscal Years 1999–2002. Further, the new law eliminates the long-standing requirement that states must provide family planning services to all cash assistance recipients who request them.

All in all, this new legislation, with its exclusive emphasis on abstinence until marriage and its deletion of funds for education about contraception, may even have the unintended effect of increasing teenage pregnancy, by ignoring the reality of adolescent sexuality and by failing to teach teens about how to prevent pregnancy and sexually transmitted diseases, particularly HIV/AIDS.

Work Opportunities for Youths

Teens and young adults need positive alternatives to too-early parenthood—real options that give them a sense of hope and of a developing path to self-sufficiency and attainment of adult roles. Part of this positive motivation should result from the development of workplace skills and a vision of a long-term career path. Yet, while 1996 brought continued economic growth and declining unemployment overall, improvements in youth unemployment were minimal. The official unemployment rate for 16- to 19-year-olds fell from 17.3 percent in 1995 to 16.7 percent in 1996. For young adults (ages 20 through 24), the unemployment rate actually edged up to 9.2 percent in 1996, from 9.1 percent in 1995. Both the teen and young adult rates remain higher than in 1990, even while the general unemployment rate is lower.

The current recovery has not brought much relief from the economic disaster that has afflicted America's younger workers and families for more than two decades. Changes in the economy have made it far harder for young people with limited education to get jobs that pay decent wages. Many schools have not responded with the improvements needed to lift the skills of more youths; the high school graduation rate has stopped increasing (see Education chapter); and the labor market has widened intergenerational economic divisions, particularly for those without college educations. The median weekly earnings of men under 25 who worked full-time were three-quarters those of older men in 1967, but barely half in 1995. Young women's earnings suffered a comparable drop in relation to those of older women. The 1996 and 1997 minimum-wage increases that Congress mandated should help, but not nearly enough.

Economics profoundly influences young people's family lives. As fewer young men have wages that are adequate to support a family, fewer get married. For more than 20 years, the proportion of young men with earnings below poverty has been rising sharply; the proportion of young men getting married has fallen sharply; and the share of young men living with their parents or other relatives (other than a wife and children) has grown. During that time, the teen birth rate has not gone up, but births to unmarried teen mothers have skyrocketed.

Drugs, Cigarettes, and Alcohol

In 1996, the government reported troubling increases in drug use, especially marijuana use, among teenagers. Use of illicit drugs in the preceding month among 12- to 17-year-olds rose from 8.2 percent in 1994 to 10.9 percent in 1995, while the rate among the overall population remained virtually flat, according to the 1995 National Household Survey on Drug Abuse. Marijuana use increased from 3.4 percent in 1992 and 6.0 percent in 1994 to 8.2 percent in 1995. This trend in illicit drug use is consistent with the results reported in the 1995 Monitoring the Future Study conducted by the National Institute on Drug Abuse, which showed statistically significant increases in drug use among eighth-, tenth-, and twelfth-graders from 1992 through 1995. The recent jump is particularly discouraging because the National Household Survey on Drug Abuse reported that past-month drug use by teenagers had declined from 16.3 percent in 1979 to 5.3 percent in 1992.

A detailed analysis of the combined 1991–1993 National Household Surveys on Drug Abuse showed that adolescents not living with two biological parents, regardless of age, gender, family income, and race or ethnicity, are 50 percent to 150 percent more likely than other adolescents to use illicit drugs, alcohol, or cigarettes, to be dependent on substances, or to report problems associated with use. For marijuana, the highest rates of use were in father-only, father/stepmother, and mother-only families (rates of 17.1 percent, 16.8 percent, and 11.4 percent, compared with 6.9 percent for families with both biological parents present). The same analysis reported that Black adolescents, regardless of family type, were less likely to have used or been dependent upon substances in the previous year than either White or Hispanic teens.

Our society gives children and adolescents mixed messages about drug use, through high rates of adult drug use (see Children and Families in Crisis chapter), and through glamorization of drug use at the same time that the drumbeat about its dangers is fading. Both the 1994 National Household Survey and the Monitoring the Future Study showed that the perceived risk of harm in using drugs had declined among youths in recent years.

Mixed messages about alcohol use and cigarette smoking also are having a negative impact. The decline in teen alcohol use documented during the 1980s and early 1990s came to a halt in 1994. Yet in 1996 a handful of liquor companies announced that they would stop adhering to the industry's 48-year-old voluntary agreement not to advertise hard liquor on television or radio. Consumer groups and children's groups objected, saying that hard liquor advertisements, especially during prime time and weekend sports events (where the ads have begun to appear), will increase youth alcohol use. Moreover, a survey by Competitive Media Reporting for the *Wall Street Journal* showed that beer commercials already appear on many youth-oriented shows, and that on several occasions during one randomly chosen week, youths under the drinking age made up the majority of the audience for beer commercials.

Hundreds of thousands of adolescents also start smoking each year—they are most likely to begin to experiment with smoking between the ages of 12 and 13—despite smoking's devastating health effects. Tobacco kills more Americans each year than alcohol, cocaine, crack, heroin, homicide, suicide, car accidents, fires, and AIDS combined, according to the Campaign for Tobacco-Free Kids. Cigarette advertising is twice as likely as peer pressure to influence teens to smoke, according to a study published in the *Journal of the National Cancer Institute* in late 1995. One of the bright spots for youth development in 1996 was ongoing public support, and support in the Clinton Administration, for the federal Food and Drug Administration's aggressive proposal to decrease smoking among children by stopping the sale and marketing of cigarettes to them.

Federal Investments in Youth Development

In 1995, the Carnegie Council on Adolescent Development's final report, *Great Transitions: Preparing Adolescents for a New Century*, warned that our society is abandoning 19 million youths "at the most crucial turning point in their passage from childhood to adulthood." Children are left at great risk of too-early pregnancy, drug and alcohol abuse, AIDS and other sexually transmitted diseases, suicide, and violence.

Nevertheless, the federal government's already-weak response to such problems was weakened further in 1996. Congress slashed to the bone youth violence and crime prevention programs created in 1994 (see Violence chapter), undercutting a wide range of community activities to help young people, and reduced a range of youth employment and training initiatives. Job Training and Partnership Act (JTPA) youth training programs, for which $599 million was appropriated in 1995, received only $127 million for Fiscal Year 1997. Rather than strongly opposing this cut, the Clinton Administration proposed a new, $250 million program that Congress did not consider seriously. Funding for the very successful YouthBuild program was cut to far below the level needed to sustain existing services, receiving for Fiscal Years 1996 and 1997 combined the same amount it originally was slated to receive in Fiscal Year 1995 alone.

Structural changes, however, were not made in federal youth development programs in 1996. Sen. Nancy Kassebaum's proposal to create a new Youth Development Community Block Grant did not pass. While that bill did highlight the need for investments in all young people, it did not add any new funds. That, along with concerns about the structure of the proposed block grant, led to its demise.

Congress did reverse its decision to cut all 1996 and 1997 funding for summer youth employment (which would have eliminated more than 600,000 summer jobs each year), and restored the funds. And the AmeriCorps program of national youth service, a priority of President Clinton's, also survived congressional attempts to eviscerate it.

The cuts and attempted cuts came despite the proven successes of many youth development programs. A 1996 evaluation by Abt Associates, for example, found youth corps programs (in which young people work in teams to perform community service, while learning discipline and skills) to be cost-effective and to have strikingly positive effects on participants, particularly 16- to 24-year-old Black males. Opportunities to learn, opportunities to contribute to the community, and constructive interactions with caring adults are all elements of a positive youth development strategy that has a real payoff.

Union Industrial Home for Children

At 14, Amesha's hope to be adopted, to stop moving from foster home to foster home, vanished when she became pregnant. Prospects for her and her unborn baby looked pretty dismal. But when a caseworker placed the Newark, N.J., teen at the Union Industrial Home for Children (UIH), Amesha's life began to turn around.

Three years later, Amesha has completed high school—unlike many teen mothers. Her son, Sha'Quil, was born healthy, thanks in part to the prenatal care she received while living at UIH, and Amesha has not become pregnant again. Amesha and Sha'Quil recently moved into a one-bedroom apartment, as part of UIH's two-year transitional housing program. She is studying respiratory therapy full-time at the nearby two-year college, while Sha'Quil attends a local day care center. With UIH's assistance, Amesha has learned to prepare a household budget, has developed effective parenting skills, and will enter the world of work independent of public assistance.

The New Empowerment Alternatives (NEA) residential program that helped Amesha is just one component of UIH's efforts. With the mission of serving children and their families in New Jersey, with priority to Mercer County, the 137-year-old UIH provides varied social services and opportunities for education and job training to prepare young people to function independently and responsibly in society.

Recognizing the importance of fathers in the lives of children, UIH also operates two programs for teen males and adult men—First Steps and Operation Fatherhood. First Steps works with 13- to 17-year-old fathers and at-risk youths. The teens, referred by the local high school and community agencies, attend weekly peer support group meetings, where they talk about their role as fathers and hold discussions on health and sexuality. First Steps also has a cultural component, in which the youths take college tours or visit museums, so they can see themselves in a larger context than the city of Trenton.

"First Steps helps young men understand that having a child is a lifetime commitment, and that they have a legal obligation as a parent," says Delores Ijames-Bryant, acting director of Operation Fatherhood. "They learn that if they are sexually active, the relationship is serious. This sexual relationship makes them potential fathers, whose lives may change suddenly and drastically."

Operation Fatherhood, begun in 1992, each year serves about 200 18- to 44-year-old noncustodial fathers of children receiving public assistance. Fathers who are in court for paternity establishment or failure to pay child support are referred to Operation Fatherhood, where they attend peer support group meetings and job-readiness classes that help them with résumé-writing and interviewing skills. Then they undertake job searches.

Most men find jobs within one to three months, and preliminary results from a 1994 Manpower Demonstration Research Corp. study confirmed that the men were keeping jobs. Once a man is employed, a UIH "job coach" checks regularly with the employer and the employee for the first six months, to make sure everything is going smoothly. A portion of each man's wages is garnisheed automatically for child support.

Operation Fatherhood men use other UIH resources, including on-the-job training help, transportation, participation in parenting groups, and weekly support groups for employed clients. On group father–child outings, such as a recent trip to the aquarium, fathers can share experiences with their children.

"Men do care, and they want to be involved with their children," says Ijames-Bryant. Understanding the child support system, engaging in positive discussions with their peers around parenting issues, getting actively involved with their children, and receiving help finding jobs that pay livable wages and enable them to fulfill their responsibilities to their children—these make all the difference in the world.

(For more information, contact Khadijah Muhammad, UIH's Residential Services director, at 609-695-1492.)

Opportunities to Help Children

We must restore to teenagers a belief in themselves, their futures, and the broader society. As long as they lack adequate opportunities to learn, work, develop healthy self-esteem, and succeed, our nation will face abnormally high rates of teen pregnancy, drug use, violence, and other risk-taking or self-destructive behaviors. Conversely, if we provide all teens opportunities to develop to their full potential, the entire society will benefit.

Building those opportunities, and bolstering teens' motivation and capacity to avoid harmful behaviors, requires a wide range of strategies. Because many problems of teens are directly linked to child poverty and school failure, if we expect teens to avoid these behaviors we must lift millions of children out of poverty (see Family Income chapter) and vastly improve America's schools, especially for minority and low-income students (see Education chapter). But we must also:

✦ Expand investments in after-school and summer programs for all teenagers, particularly those in low-income neighborhoods. These recreational and enrichment programs in structured, supervised settings can pay big dividends in reducing risk-taking behavior (see Children, Violence, and Crime chapter). The funding that was set aside in the 1994 crime law for these purposes should be restored to its intended use.

✦ Expand mentoring and tutoring projects in every community, using civic groups, congregations, youth-serving organizations, fraternities and sororities, and other community-based organizations.

✦ Strengthen age-appropriate family life education and comprehensive school-based or school-linked services that promote adolescent health and pregnancy prevention. Extensive parent involvement and close work with education, health, and other officials are essential to build effective programs that respond appropriately to teens' needs and have strong local consensus behind them.

✦ Expand youth employment opportunities through successful programs like Job Corps, YouthBuild, youth corps, and others. Cuts in summer youth employment, job training, and national service programs for poor and minority teenagers should be resisted.

Finally, we all need to begin to support and nurture teenagers far more, and to fear and stigmatize them far less. Many of us too casually have become willing to hold teenagers to adult standards of behavior and punish them as adults, but not give them the supports, guidance, and adult supervision that recognize they are still children in the process of becoming adults. Teens must be responsible for their behavior, but the society must be responsible for giving teens the capacity and motivation to behave as we expect.

Appendix

Children in the Nation

TABLE A1.
A Profile of America's Children
March 1996

Percent of children under 18	Total	White	Black	American Indian	Asian American	Hispanic
Living with both parents	71.6%	78.0%	38.7%	57.1%	84.0%	67.2%
Living with only a father	3.4	3.3	3.9	6.0	3.1	3.2
Living with only a mother	24.2	17.9	56.9	36.5	12.5	28.6
Living with grandparents only	2.0	1.4	5.4	3.5	0.9	2.4
Who are foster children	0.6	0.5	1.3	1.1	0.2	0.7
With a grandparent in the home	8.0	6.1	15.7	11.9	13.4	10.2
Received some child support in 1955	12.5	12.4	14.4	15.6	4.7	7.9
Parents own their home	56.9	63.4	28.2	35.9	50.3	33.4
Family had earnings in 1995	92.1	94.7	80.7	85.5	88.8	86.4
At least one parent at work	84.1	88.5	64.9	73.5	79.7	75.4
A parent unemployed	6.5	5.8	9.4	12.9	6.0	10.5
Whose mother works	59.6	61.1	53.7	54.1	55.9	43.3
Father works, mother at home	20.4	23.2	7.7	12.4	20.4	27.4
A parent completed college	27.7	30.0	13.2	15.2	45.2	8.1
Neither parent is a HS graduate	14.7	12.6	23.9	23.4	16.2	43.9
Child is not a citizen	3.4	2.8	1.9	1.2	21.3	12.1
Living below poverty	20.5	16.0	41.3	41.4	19.2	39.5
Living above poverty and below 4 times poverty	56.8	58.8	49.4	48.4	51.3	53.9
Living over 4 times poverty	22.6	25.2	9.3	10.1	29.4	6.6
Living in central city	24.7	19.1	48.1	27.5	38.1	40.0
Covered by private health insurance	66.1	71.0	43.9	44.6	67.2	38.3
Covered by employer-provided health insurance	61.6	66.0	41.6	42.9	61.3	36.7
Covered by Medicaid	23.2	18.3	45.4	51.8	21.9	37.4
Covered by any health insurance	86.2	86.6	84.7	86.3	86.0	73.2
Without health insurance	13.8	13.4	15.3	13.7	14.0	26.8
Family received food stamps in 1995	18.1	13.5	40.3	33.2	14.8	31.6
Family received SSI benefits in 1995	4.2	2.8	9.5	5.1	8.9	4.8
Family received AFDC/General Assistance in 1995	12.6	8.7	30.5	24.6	12.9	21.5

Notes: Hispanic persons may be of any race. Estimates for American Indian and Asian American children are based on small samples. Parents include step-, foster, and grandparents; children living with only grandparents also are shown separately.

Weighted average poverty thresholds in 1995 were $12,158 for three-person families and $15,569 for four-person families.

Employment and unemployment data reflect family status at time of survey. Other data reflect family status for full year or any time during the year.

Source: U.S. Department of Commerce, Bureau of the Census, March 1996 *Current Population Survey.*

National Trends

TABLE A2.
Poverty Among Children*

Year	Number of Children Under 18 Who Are Poor	Child Poverty Rate	Number of Children Under 6 Who Are Poor	Poverty Rate for Children Under 6
1959	17,552,000	27.3%	n/a	n/a
1960	17,634,000	26.9	n/a	n/a
1961	16,909,000	25.6	n/a	n/a
1962	16,963,000	25.0	n/a	n/a
1963	16,005,000	23.1	n/a	n/a
1964	16,051,000	23.0	n/a	n/a
1965	14,676,000	21.0	n/a	n/a
1966	12,389,000	17.6	n/a	n/a
1967	11,656,000	16.6	n/a	n/a
1968	10,954,000	15.6	n/a	n/a
1969	9,691,000	14.0	3,298,000	15.3%
1970	10,440,000	15.1	3,561,000	16.6
1971	10,551,000	15.3	3,499,000	16.9
1972	10,284,000	15.1	3,276,000	16.1
1973	9,642,000	14.4	3,097,000	15.7
1974	10,156,000	15.4	3,294,000	16.9
1975	11,104,000	17.1	3,460,000	18.2
1976	10,273,000	16.0	3,270,000	17.7
1977	10,288,000	16.2	3,326,000	18.1
1978	9,931,000	15.9	3,184,000	17.2
1979	10,377,000	16.4	3,415,000	17.8
1980	11,543,000	18.3	4,030,000	20.5
1981	12,505,000	20.0	4,422,000	22.0
1982	13,647,000	21.9	4,821,000	23.3
1983	13,911,000	22.3	5,122,000	24.6
1984	13,420,000	21.5	4,938,000	23.4
1985	13,010,000	20.7	4,832,000	22.6
1986	12,876,000	20.5	4,619,000	21.6
1987	12,843,000	20.3	4,852,000	22.4
1988	12,455,000	19.5	5,032,000	22.6
1989	12,590,000	19.6	5,071,000	22.5
1990	13,431,000	20.6	5,198,000	23.0
1991	14,341,000	21.8	5,483,000	24.0
1992	14,617,000	21.9	5,781,000	25.0
1993	14,961,000	22.0	6,097,000	25.6
1994	14,610,000	21.2	5,878,000	24.5
1995	13,999,000	20.2	5,670,000	23.7

*Related children in families. This definition excludes persons under18 who are married, parents, or living on their own.
n/a Data not available.

Source: U.S. Department of Commerce, Bureau of the Census.

TABLE A3.
Maternal and Infant Health

Year	Infant Mortality Rates*				Low Birth-weight**	Percent of Babies Born to Mothers Who Received Late*** or No Prenatal Care		
	Total	White	Black	Black-White Ratio		Total	White	Black
1940	47.0	43.2	72.9	1.69	n/a	n/a	n/a	n/a
1950	29.2	26.8	43.9	1.64	n/a	n/a	n/a	n/a
1959	26.4	23.2	44.8	1.93	n/a	n/a	n/a	n/a
1960	26.0	22.9	44.3	1.93	7.7%	n/a	n/a	n/a
1961	25.3	22.4	41.8	1.87	7.8	n/a	n/a	n/a
1962	25.3	22.3	42.6	1.91	8.0	n/a	n/a	n/a
1963	25.2	22.2	42.8	1.93	8.2	n/a	n/a	n/a
1964	24.8	21.6	42.3	1.96	8.2	n/a	n/a	n/a
1965	24.7	21.5	41.7	1.94	8.3	n/a	n/a	n/a
1966	23.7	20.6	40.2	1.95	8.3	n/a	n/a	n/a
1967	22.4	19.7	37.5	1.90	8.2	n/a	n/a	n/a
1968	21.8	19.2	36.2	1.89	8.2	n/a	n/a	n/a
1969	20.9	18.4	34.8	1.89	8.1	8.1%	6.3%	18.2%
1970	20.0	17.8	32.6	1.83	7.9	7.9	6.2	16.6
1971	19.1	17.1	30.3	1.77	7.7	7.2	5.8	14.6
1972	18.5	16.4	29.6	1.80	7.7	7.0	5.5	13.2
1973	17.7	15.8	28.1	1.78	7.6	6.7	5.4	12.4
1974	16.7	14.8	26.8	1.81	7.4	6.2	5.0	11.4
1975	16.1	14.2	26.2	1.85	7.4	6.0	5.0	10.5
1976	15.2	13.3	25.5	1.92	7.3	5.7	4.8	9.9
1977	14.1	12.3	23.6	1.92	7.1	5.6	4.7	9.6
1978	13.8	12.0	23.1	1.93	7.1	5.4	4.5	9.3
1979	13.1	11.4	21.8	1.91	6.9	5.1	4.3	8.9
1980	12.6	10.9	22.2	2.04	6.8	5.1	4.3	8.8
1981	11.9	10.3	20.8	2.02	6.8	5.2	4.3	9.1
1982	11.5	9.9	20.5	2.07	6.8	5.5	4.5	9.6
1983	11.2	9.6	20.0	2.08	6.8	5.6	4.6	9.7
1984	10.8	9.3	19.2	2.06	6.7	5.6	4.7	9.6
1985	10.6	9.2	19.0	2.07	6.8	5.7	4.7	10.0
1986	10.4	8.8	18.9	2.15	6.8	6.0	5.0	10.6
1987	10.1	8.5	18.8	2.21	6.9	6.1	5.0	11.1
1988	10.0	8.4	18.5	2.20	6.9	6.1	5.0	10.9
1989	9.8	8.1	18.6	2.30	7.0	6.4	5.2	11.9
1990	9.2	7.6	18.0	2.37	7.0	6.1	4.9	11.3
1991	8.9	7.3	17.6	2.41	7.1	5.8	4.7	10.7
1992	8.5	6.9	16.8	2.43	7.1	5.2	4.2	9.9
1993	8.4	6.8	16.5	2.43	7.2	4.8	3.9	9.0
1994	8.0	6.6	15.8	2.39	7.3	4.4	3.6	8.2

*Infant deaths before the first birthday per 1,000 live births.
**Birthweight less than 2,500 grams (5 lbs., 8 oz.).
***Prenatal care begun in the last three months of pregnancy.
n/a Data not available.

Source: U.S. Department of Health and Human Services, National Center for Health Statistics.

TABLE A4.
Adolescent Childbearing

Year	Total Fertility Rate*	Total Unmarried Birth Rate**	Teen Fertility Rate***	Teen Unmarried Birth Rate****
1959	118.8	21.9	89.1	15.5
1960	118.0	21.6	89.1	15.3
1961	117.1	22.7	88.6	16.0
1962	112.0	21.9	81.4	14.8
1963	108.3	22.5	76.7	15.3
1964	104.7	23.0	73.1	15.9
1965	96.3	23.5	70.5	16.7
1966	90.8	23.4	70.3	17.5
1967	87.2	23.9	67.5	18.5
1968	85.2	24.4	65.6	19.7
1969	86.1	25.0	65.5	20.4
1970	87.9	26.4	68.3	22.4
1971	81.6	25.5	64.5	22.3
1972	73.1	24.8	61.7	22.8
1973	68.8	24.3	59.3	22.7
1974	67.8	23.9	57.5	23.0
1975	66.0	24.5	55.6	23.9
1976	65.0	24.3	52.8	23.7
1977	66.8	25.6	52.8	25.1
1978	65.5	25.7	51.5	24.9
1979	67.2	27.2	52.3	26.4
1980	68.4	29.4	53.0	27.6
1981	67.4	29.5	52.2	27.9
1982	67.3	30.0	52.4	28.7
1983	65.8	30.3	51.4	29.5
1984	65.4	31.0	50.6	30.0
1985	66.2	32.8	51.0	31.4
1986	65.4	34.2	50.2	32.3
1987	65.7	36.0	50.6	33.8
1988	67.2	38.5	53.0	36.4
1989	69.2	41.6	57.3	40.1
1990	70.9	43.8	59.9	42.5
1991	69.6	45.2	62.1	44.8
1992	68.9	45.2	60.7	44.6
1993	67.6	45.3	59.6	44.5
1994	66.7	46.9	58.9	46.4

*Births per 1,000 females ages 15-44.
**Births per 1,000 unmarried females ages 15-44.
***Births per 1,000 females ages 15-19.
****Births per 1,000 unmarried females ages 15-19.

Source: U.S. Department of Health and Human Services, National Center for Health Statistics.

TABLE A5.
Youth Unemployment

Year	Total Unemployment Rates			Unemployment Rates, Youths Not Enrolled in School		
				Level of Education		
	All Ages	Age 16-19	Age 20-24	Less Than Four Years of High School	High School Graduate Only	Four Years or More of College
1959	5.5%	14.6%	8.5%	n/a	n/a	n/a
1960	5.5	14.7	8.7	n/a	n/a	n/a
1961	6.7	16.8	10.4	n/a	n/a	n/a
1962	5.5	14.7	9.0	n/a	n/a	n/a
1963	5.7	17.2	8.8	n/a	n/a	n/a
1964	5.2	16.2	8.3	n/a	n/a	n/a
1965	4.5	14.8	6.7	n/a	n/a	n/a
1966	3.8	12.8	5.3	n/a	n/a	n/a
1967	3.8	12.9	5.7	n/a	n/a	n/a
1968	3.6	12.7	5.8	n/a	n/a	n/a
1969	3.5	12.2	5.7	n/a	n/a	n/a
1970	4.9	15.3	8.2	17.2%	9.9%	6.5%
1971	5.9	16.9	10.0	18.0	9.6	6.6
1972	5.6	16.2	9.3	16.8	9.5	7.2
1973	4.9	14.5	7.8	14.9	7.2	4.9
1974	5.6	16.0	9.1	19.2	9.8	5.0
1975	8.5	19.9	13.6	25.3	13.6	8.2
1976	7.7	19.0	12.0	24.7	12.1	7.1
1977	7.1	17.8	11.0	20.6	10.5	8.0
1978	6.1	16.4	9.6	18.8	8.8	6.3
1979	5.8	16.1	9.1	19.2	9.9	5.0
1980	7.1	17.8	11.5	25.3	12.5	5.9
1981	7.6	19.6	12.3	26.9	13.8	5.3
1982	9.7	23.2	14.9	31.8	17.3	9.2
1983	9.6	22.4	14.5	27.3	15.2	7.0
1984	7.5	18.9	11.5	25.8	11.8	5.9
1985	7.2	18.6	11.1	25.9	12.7	5.4
1986	7.0	18.3	10.7	24.3	11.5	4.8
1987	6.2	16.9	9.7	21.8	10.7	5.5
1988	5.5	15.3	8.7	20.0	10.1	4.8
1989	5.3	15.0	8.6	19.9	10.1	5.0
1990	5.5	15.5	8.8	20.0	10.4	5.2
1991	6.7	18.6	10.8	23.1	12.7	6.9
1992	7.4	20.0	11.3	24.9	13.9	6.5
1993	6.8	19.0	10.5	22.8	13.1	6.1
1994	6.1	17.6	9.7	23.1	11.9	5.5
1995	5.6	17.3	9.1	21.5	12.2	5.6

n/a Data not available.

Source: U.S. Department of Labor, Bureau of Labor Statistics.

Children in the States

TABLE B1.

Number and Percentage of Children Under 18
Who Are Poor, Based on 1989 Income

	All Races		White		Black		Hispanic	
	Number	Percent	Number	Percent	Number	Percent	Number	Percent
Alabama	253,636	24.2%	89,959	12.9%	160,510	47.5%	1,829	23.4%
Alaska	19,284	11.4	8,864	7.4	1,086	14.5	809	12.2
Arizona	212,001	22.0	104,283	14.9	12,813	35.7	89,883	34.9
Arkansas	155,399	25.3	82,932	17.7	70,023	52.0	2,290	31.9
California	1,380,275	18.2	591,097	12.7	195,563	30.7	713,980	27.2
Colorado	129,565	15.3	88,222	12.2	13,677	33.8	48,497	32.7
Connecticut	79,020	10.7	36,963	6.1	23,591	28.9	30,002	41.2
Delaware	19,256	12.0	7,543	6.3	10,600	30.8	1,297	25.0
District of Columbia	28,610	25.5	799	4.9	26,339	29.1	1,677	26.3
Florida	525,446	18.7	252,793	12.0	243,435	41.0	93,288	24.6
Georgia	343,068	20.1	108,825	9.9	227,207	40.0	7,163	24.0
Hawaii	31,944	11.6	8,306	9.9	969	11.7	5,296	17.8
Idaho	49,159	16.2	41,528	14.7	281	22.5	7,705	35.4
Illinois	495,505	17.0	204,276	9.7	233,506	43.3	80,047	25.0
Indiana	203,791	14.2	141,319	11.2	55,984	40.1	7,627	21.8
Iowa	101,661	14.3	89,059	13.1	8,241	50.6	3,253	26.7
Kansas	93,066	14.3	65,528	11.5	18,665	40.3	8,233	23.5
Kentucky	234,012	24.8	193,614	22.7	38,193	47.0	1,803	26.2
Louisiana	380,942	31.4	112,404	15.4	259,228	56.5	5,908	23.3
Maine	41,897	13.8	40,429	13.6	440	25.9	435	16.2
Maryland	128,523	11.3	46,164	6.1	77,002	23.2	4,165	12.3
Massachusetts	176,221	13.2	105,129	9.2	29,547	33.3	49,645	49.1
Michigan	450,426	18.6	239,263	12.4	188,405	46.2	22,103	30.2
Minnesota	146,386	12.7	102,624	9.7	17,394	49.5	6,486	30.7
Mississippi	248,705	33.6	59,138	14.9	186,212	55.6	1,471	30.9
Missouri	230,058	17.7	152,757	13.9	71,928	41.5	4,246	20.3
Montana	44,706	20.5	33,458	17.1	221	31.1	1,874	36.0
Nebraska	58,474	13.8	44,420	11.4	8,761	43.2	3,861	27.9
Nevada	38,232	13.3	22,893	9.9	8,358	33.5	8,491	21.5
New Hampshire	20,440	7.4	19,295	7.2	351	15.3	705	16.4
New Jersey	200,726	11.3	84,110	6.4	81,788	27.8	59,531	27.8
New Mexico	122,260	27.8	67,615	22.1	3,542	35.0	70,158	35.0
New York	799,531	19.1	342,541	11.9	274,947	34.1	269,703	41.9
North Carolina	272,923	17.2	102,034	9.3	158,007	35.9	5,047	24.2
North Dakota	29,732	17.1	23,031	14.4	204	15.1	623	27.5
Ohio	493,206	17.8	315,714	13.4	163,131	45.4	15,910	32.0
Oklahoma	179,283	21.7	105,173	16.6	34,475	44.5	11,950	35.8
Oregon	111,629	15.8	91,249	14.2	5,489	36.3	14,285	33.8
Pennsylvania	432,227	15.7	270,941	11.5	124,859	40.6	38,374	46.7
Rhode Island	30,842	13.8	20,274	10.4	4,425	35.9	6,356	41.3
South Carolina	190,873	21.0	52,430	9.5	136,563	39.6	1,635	19.0
South Dakota	39,896	20.4	25,008	14.7	327	26.7	663	27.8
Tennessee	251,529	21.0	142,418	15.2	106,024	43.0	2,400	24.1
Texas	1,159,710	24.3	612,724	18.3	254,287	39.3	638,905	40.2
Utah	78,041	12.5	64,755	11.1	1,290	34.7	9,213	26.8
Vermont	17,020	12.0	16,435	11.9	211	24.9	143	11.8
Virginia	197,382	13.3	88,370	8.1	102,862	30.9	5,147	11.9
Washington	179,272	14.5	124,632	11.9	14,548	30.5	27,381	34.0
West Virginia	115,073	26.2	106,458	25.4	7,887	50.2	814	34.3
Wisconsin	188,863	14.9	110,939	9.9	53,392	55.8	12,435	33.7
Wyoming	19,190	14.4	15,532	12.6	340	31.5	2,724	28.1
United States	11,428,916	18.3%	5,876,267	12.5%	3,717,128	39.8%	2,407,466	32.2%

Note: Persons of Hispanic origin can be of any race.

TABLE B1.

Number and Percentage of Children Under 18
Who Are Poor, Based on 1989 Income (continued)

	Native American		Asian/Pacific Islander		Other	
	Number	Percent	Number	Percent	Number	Percent
Alabama	1,519	24.6%	1,166	19.0%	482	28.0%
Alaska	8,621	25.7	500	8.3	213	12.6
Arizona	44,607	53.1	2,204	14.9	48,094	38.2
Arkansas	1,053	26.1	648	17.5	743	34.7
California	17,982	26.5	155,493	19.6	420,140	30.2
Colorado	3,008	35.4	3,130	17.6	21,528	36.8
Connecticut	313	21.4	917	6.6	17,236	47.1
Delaware	80	21.5	149	6.6	884	30.0
District of Columbia	55	35.7	232	16.0	1,185	31.6
Florida	2,541	26.1	5,194	12.9	21,483	31.5
Georgia	938	25.0	2,465	11.5	3,633	29.7
Hawaii	408	25.2	21,327	12.1	934	16.5
Idaho	2,056	40.5	567	20.6	4,727	40.9
Illinois	1,422	23.9	7,640	9.4	48,661	27.8
Indiana	1,132	30.2	1,124	11.6	4,232	27.8
Iowa	1,160	43.4	1,898	23.5	1,303	28.4
Kansas	1,932	26.8	2,203	22.2	4,738	26.6
Kentucky	681	41.8	867	16.5	657	26.2
Louisiana	3,166	46.9	4,414	34.0	1,730	30.3
Maine	583	28.3	326	13.6	119	19.0
Maryland	661	18.5	2,820	7.6	1,876	14.3
Massachusetts	1,309	35.3	9,330	24.1	30,906	51.9
Michigan	6,147	32.5	4,891	14.6	11,720	35.9
Minnesota	10,459	54.8	12,638	37.1	3,271	37.5
Mississippi	1,429	45.6	1,657	39.7	269	32.5
Missouri	1,483	26.2	1,984	17.7	1,906	25.0
Montana	10,238	53.4	224	17.6	565	43.3
Nebraska	2,795	57.0	724	17.9	1,774	31.8
Nevada	1,745	29.8	1,040	10.9	4,196	25.0
New Hampshire	119	25.6	370	13.4	305	22.6
New Jersey	886	26.2	4,622	5.9	29,320	33.0
New Mexico	26,643	50.1	797	18.4	23,663	36.0
New York	4,800	29.6	25,021	14.9	152,222	47.6
North Carolina	7,820	29.9	2,344	16.4	2,718	31.2
North Dakota	6,179	58.3	148	16.8	170	22.6
Ohio	1,588	30.4	3,557	14.1	9,216	39.3
Oklahoma	31,977	34.8	1,427	15.8	6,231	40.4
Oregon	4,288	32.3	3,752	19.2	6,851	37.2
Pennsylvania	1,128	31.1	8,354	20.7	26,945	54.7
Rhode Island	440	39.5	2,043	34.0	3,660	42.5
South Carolina	599	27.4	715	12.1	566	21.6
South Dakota	14,160	63.3	195	17.0	206	26.2
Tennessee	906	30.8	1,438	15.7	743	25.8
Texas	4,501	25.6	14,518	15.6	273,680	40.6
Utah	4,893	47.3	2,281	19.8	4,822	33.5
Vermont	251	36.3	70	7.3	53	20.2
Virginia	666	19.0	3,377	7.8	2,107	13.5
Washington	10,228	37.7	12,594	20.0	17,270	39.8
West Virginia	337	44.6	193	8.5	198	32.1
Wisconsin	6,505	46.1	10,819	48.8	7,208	42.5
Wyoming	1,966	49.0	84	10.0	1,268	35.2
United States	260,403	38.8%	346,491	17.1%	1,228,627	35.5%

Source: U.S. Department of Commerce, Bureau of the Census, 1990 Census of Population and Housing, Summary Tape File 3. Calculations by Children's Defense Fund.

TABLE B2.

AFDC and Food Stamp Benefits for a Three-Person Family, 1996

	Maximum Monthly AFDC Benefit					AFDC and Food Stamp Benefits as a Percent of Poverty, 1996			
	1970 Maximum (Actual Dollars)	1970 Adjusted for Inflation	1996 Actual Maximum	Percent Change 1970– 1996	Rank	Combined Percent	Combined Rank	AFDC Percent	AFDC Rank
Alabama	$ 65	$ 257	$164	−36.2%	11	44.1%	50	15.2%	50
Alaska	328	1,299	923	−28.9	5	92.0	2	68.3	1
Arizona	138	546	347	−36.4	12	61.0	33	32.1	33
Arkansas	89	352	204	−42.0	20	47.8	45	18.9	45
California	186	736	607	−17.5	1	78.8	6	56.1	5
Colorado	193	764	421	−44.9	23	66.7	22	38.9	22
Connecticut	283	1,120	636	−43.2	21	80.6	4	58.8	3
Delaware	160	633	338	−46.6	31	60.2	35	31.2	35
District of Columbia	195	772	420	−45.6	25	66.7	22	38.8	24
Florida	114	451	303	−32.8	8	56.9	38	28.0	38
Georgia	107	424	280	−34.0	9	54.8	41	25.9	41
Hawaii	226	895	712	−20.4	2	95.1	1	57.2	4
Idaho	211	835	317	−62.0	49	58.2	36	29.3	36
Illinois	232	918	377	−58.9	45	63.8	27	34.9	27
Indiana	120	475	288	−39.4	17	55.6	40	26.6	40
Iowa	201	796	426	−46.5	28	67.0	19	39.4	18
Kansas	222	879	429	−51.2	40	68.6	15	39.7	17
Kentucky	147	582	262	−55.0	42	53.2	43	24.2	43
Louisiana	88	348	190	−45.4	24	46.5	47	17.6	47
Maine	135	534	418	−21.7	3	66.5	25	38.6	25
Maryland	162	641	373	−41.8	19	63.4	28	34.5	28
Massachusetts	268	1,061	565	−46.7	32	76.0	9	52.2	7
Michigan	219	867	459	−47.1	35	69.2	14	42.4	14
Minnesota	256	1,013	532	−47.5	36	73.9	11	49.2	11
Mississippi	56	222	120	−45.9	26	40.0	51	11.1	51
Missouri	104	412	292	−29.1	7	55.9	39	27.0	39
Montana	202	800	425	−46.9	33	66.9	21	39.3	20
Nebraska	171	677	364	−46.2	27	62.6	29	33.7	29
Nevada	121	479	348	−27.3	4	61.1	32	32.2	32
New Hampshire	262	1,037	550	−47.0	34	75.1	10	50.8	9
New Jersey	302	1,196	424	−64.5	50	67.6	16	39.2	21
New Mexico	149	590	389	−34.1	10	64.6	26	36.0	26
New York	279	1,105	577	−47.8	37	78.3	7	53.3	6
North Carolina	145	574	272	−52.6	41	54.1	42	25.1	42
North Dakota	213	843	431	−48.9	38	67.4	17	39.8	15
Ohio	161	637	341	−46.5	28	60.5	34	31.5	34
Oklahoma	152	602	307	−49.0	39	57.3	37	28.4	37
Oregon	184	728	460	−36.8	13	71.5	13	42.5	13
Pennsylvania	265	1,049	421	−59.9	47	66.7	22	38.9	22
Rhode Island	229	907	554	−38.9	16	78.9	5	51.2	8
South Carolina	85	337	200	−40.7	18	47.4	46	18.5	46
South Dakota	264	1,045	430	−58.9	45	67.3	18	39.8	15
Tennessee	112	443	185	−58.2	44	46.0	49	17.1	49
Texas	148	586	188	−67.9	51	46.3	48	17.4	48
Utah	175	693	426	−38.5	15	67.0	19	39.4	18
Vermont	267	1,057	656	−37.9	14	81.5	3	60.6	2
Virginia	225	891	354	−60.3	48	61.7	31	32.7	31
Washington	258	1,021	546	−46.5	28	77.2	8	50.5	10
West Virginia	114	451	253	−43.9	22	52.3	44	23.4	44
Wisconsin	184	728	517	−29.0	6	72.9	12	47.8	12
Wyoming	213	843	360	−57.3	43	62.2	30	33.3	30

Source: Congressional Research Service. Calculations by Children's Defense Fund.

TABLE B3.

Child Support Enforcement, FY 1994

	Total Caseload	Cases with Collection	Percent of Cases with Collection	Rank
Alabama	333,300	73,888	22.2%	21
Alaska	50,566	8,807	17.4	31
Arizona	307,060	17,185	5.6	51
Arkansas	127,324	30,685	24.1	17
California	2,135,813	274,622	12.9	44
Colorado	188,500	26,919	14.3	41
Connecticut	212,322	33,251	15.7	36
Delaware	51,170	14,016	27.4	12
District of Columbia	86,391	9,320	10.8	46
Florida	964,827	148,997	15.4	38
Georgia	542,578	94,303	17.4	31
Hawaii	65,007	19,079	29.3	9
Idaho	54,613	17,491	32.0	6
Illinois	726,406	73,338	10.1	48
Indiana	832,766	71,590	8.6	50
Iowa	168,229	35,870	21.3	22
Kansas	125,082	39,399	31.5	7
Kentucky	295,474	48,119	16.3	35
Louisiana	328,609	45,489	13.8	43
Maine	72,906	23,850	32.7	5
Maryland	337,874	79,357	23.5	18
Massachusetts	226,553	57,567	25.4	14
Michigan	1,416,756	222,836	15.7	36
Minnesota	212,707	81,809	38.5	1
Mississippi	268,822	31,572	11.7	45
Missouri	355,589	66,052	18.6	30
Montana	41,514	7,853	18.9	28
Nebraska	134,049	27,162	20.3	23
Nevada	77,992	15,113	19.4	26
New Hampshire	43,069	14,773	34.3	4
New Jersey	551,187	124,396	22.6	19
New Mexico	79,381	11,756	14.8	40
New York	1,227,253	187,157	15.3	39
North Carolina	447,281	90,296	20.2	24
North Dakota	37,426	8,445	22.6	19
Ohio	931,463	232,015	24.9	16
Oklahoma	123,348	20,538	16.7	33
Oregon	240,968	44,942	18.7	29
Pennsylvania	959,994	276,288	28.8	10
Rhode Island	83,763	8,577	10.2	47
South Carolina	214,060	53,703	25.1	15
South Dakota	29,398	8,457	28.8	10
Tennessee	616,373	62,431	10.1	48
Texas	732,983	121,859	16.6	34
Utah	95,613	18,822	19.7	25
Vermont	19,386	6,072	31.3	8
Virginia	360,564	68,891	19.1	27
Washington	337,639	121,079	35.9	3
West Virginia	91,050	24,548	27.0	13
Wisconsin	403,132	148,872	36.9	2
Wyoming	27,581	3,830	13.9	42
United States	18,393,711	3,353,286	18.2%	

TABLE B4.

Early Prenatal Care and Low Birthweight, 1994

	Incidence of Early* Prenatal Care, by Race of Mother						Incidence of Low-Birthweight** Births, by Race of Mother					
	All Races		White		Black		All Races		White		Black	
	Rate	Rank	Rate	Rank	Rate	Rank	Rate	Rank	Rate	Rank	Rate	Rank
Alabama	81.3%	32	87.6%	8	69.2%	29	9.0%	47	6.9%	44	13.2%	27
Alaska	84.6	10	86.3	20	85.6	2	5.5	5	5.0	1	10.7	5
Arizona	71.6	49	73.0	50	69.3	26	6.8	20	6.6	38	12.8	21
Arkansas	75.0	48	79.1	45	61.2	47	8.2	40	6.8	43	12.8	21
California	77.7	41	77.5	47	75.5	11	6.2	14	5.5	8	12.5	15
Colorado	80.7	34	81.6	40	69.9	23	8.5	41	8.1	50	15.5	42
Connecticut	88.5	5	90.4	4	76.3	9	6.9	22	6.0	21	12.7	20
Delaware	83.0	17	87.3	10	68.5	32	7.4	27	6.0	21	11.6	7
District of Columbia	57.3	51	84.3	33	53.1	50	14.2	51	5.3	7	16.1	43
Florida	81.2	33	84.8	29	69.4	24	7.7	36	6.3	32	12.5	15
Georgia	81.9	26	87.1	12	72.6	15	8.6	43	6.3	32	12.8	21
Hawaii	84.3	12	87.3	10	84.3	4	7.2	25	5.8	14	11.9	9
Idaho	78.9	40	79.2	44	80.6	5	5.5	5	5.5	8	—	—
Illinois	80.3	36	84.3	33	66.0	35	7.9	39	5.9	17	14.8	41
Indiana	80.6	35	82.5	39	64.7	39	6.8	20	6.2	27	12.4	12
Iowa	87.3	6	87.9	7	71.4	16	5.9	9	5.6	11	13.2	27
Kansas	84.6	10	85.9	24	73.1	14	6.5	18	5.9	17	12.5	15
Kentucky	83.0	17	84.4	32	69.3	26	7.7	36	7.2	47	12.4	12
Louisiana	79.2	38	87.0	13	68.7	31	9.6	49	6.4	35	14.1	35
Maine	89.4	1	89.6	5	75.0	12	5.7	7	5.8	14	—	—
Maryland	86.5	7	91.3	1	76.8	8	8.5	41	6.2	27	13.0	26
Massachusetts	89.0	3	90.6	3	78.0	6	6.4	16	5.8	14	11.0	6
Michigan	82.5	22	86.0	22	68.1	34	7.8	38	6.1	25	14.4	38
Minnesota	83.0	17	86.0	22	58.0	49	5.7	7	5.2	6	12.4	12
Mississippi	75.9	44	85.7	25	65.1	36	9.9	50	6.7	40	13.3	30
Missouri	83.9	14	86.6	17	70.1	21	7.6	32	6.4	35	13.5	31
Montana	81.6	31	84.0	36	84.4	3	6.2	14	6.3	32	—	—
Nebraska	83.4	15	84.6	30	69.4	24	6.1	13	5.7	13	12.9	25
Nevada	75.1	47	76.3	48	64.6	40	7.6	32	6.9	44	14.2	36
New Hampshire	88.6	4	88.7	6	73.3	13	5.1	1	5.1	3	—	—
New Jersey	82.2	25	86.5	18	65.0	37	7.6	32	6.1	25	13.5	31
New Mexico	66.9	50	69.5	51	58.9	48	7.3	26	7.5	49	9.1	1
New York	75.6	45	79.8	42	61.3	46	7.6	32	6.2	27	12.6	19
North Carolina	81.9	26	87.4	9	68.4	33	8.7	44	6.7	40	13.6	33
North Dakota	83.0	17	84.5	31	88.2	1	5.4	4	5.1	3	—	—
Ohio	84.0	13	86.7	16	69.1	30	7.5	29	6.4	35	13.6	33
Oklahoma	76.1	42	79.1	45	63.4	42	7.0	23	6.6	38	12.2	11
Oregon	79.1	39	79.6	43	71.2	17	5.3	2	5.1	3	10.2	4
Pennsylvania	81.8	28	85.6	26	61.4	45	7.4	27	6.2	27	14.4	38
Rhode Island	89.4	1	90.8	2	77.3	7	6.5	18	6.0	21	11.6	7
South Carolina	76.1	42	84.2	35	62.9	44	9.2	48	6.7	40	13.2	27
South Dakota	81.8	28	85.2	28	70.0	22	5.9	9	5.6	11	—	—
Tennessee	81.8	28	85.5	27	69.3	26	8.8	45	7.1	46	14.6	40
Texas	75.5	46	76.1	49	70.4	19	7.0	23	6.2	27	12.8	21
Utah	85.5	9	86.4	19	70.3	20	5.9	9	5.9	17	10.1	2
Vermont	86.0	8	86.3	20	—	—	6.0	12	5.9	17	—	—
Virginia	82.9	21	87.0	13	70.8	18	7.5	29	6.0	21	12.5	15
Washington	82.5	22	83.4	37	75.6	10	5.3	2	5.0	1	10.1	2
West Virginia	80.0	37	80.6	41	65.0	37	7.5	29	7.3	48	12.0	10
Wisconsin	83.3	16	86.8	15	63.1	43	6.4	16	5.5	8	14.3	37
Wyoming	82.3	24	83.2	38	63.9	41	8.8	45	8.8	51	—	—
United States	80.2%		82.8%		68.3%		7.3%		6.1%		13.2%	

*Care begun in the first trimester (first three months) of pregnancy.
**Less than 2,500 grams (5 lbs. 8 oz.).
— Number too small to calculate a reliable rate.

Source: U.S. Department of Health and Human Services, National Center for Health Statistics. Calculations by Children's Defense Fund.

TABLE B5.

Infant Mortality Rates,*
by Race of Mother, 1994

	All Races		White		Black	
	Rate	Rank	Rate	Rank	Rate	Rank
Alabama	10.1	47	7.0	34	16.4	19
Alaska	7.6	22	6.9	31	—	—
Arizona	7.8	26	7.4	42	16.5	20
Arkansas	9.2	42	8.2	48	13.0	4
California	7.0	13	6.5	19	15.2	13
Colorado	7.0	13	6.4	15	20.2	30
Connecticut	7.9	29	6.5	19	18.3	24
Delaware	6.8	11	5.1	2	—	—
District of Columbia	18.2	51	—	—	20.9	32
Florida	8.1	31	6.5	19	13.9	5
Georgia	10.2	48	7.1	36	16.1	16
Hawaii	6.7	8	—	—	—	—
Idaho	6.9	12	6.7	28	—	—
Illinois	9.3	43	6.8	29	18.7	27
Indiana	8.8	39	7.6	44	19.5	29
Iowa	7.5	20	7.0	34	—	—
Kansas	7.7	23	6.9	31	15.9	14
Kentucky	7.8	26	7.1	36	14.7	8
Louisiana	10.6	49	6.8	29	16.0	15
Maine	6.2	3	6.0	6	—	—
Maryland	9.0	41	6.2	10	14.7	8
Massachusetts	6.0	2	5.6	3	11.0	1
Michigan	8.6	37	6.3	13	19.3	28
Minnesota	7.0	13	6.2	10	18.6	25
Mississippi	11.0	50	7.3	41	14.7	8
Missouri	8.1	31	6.6	24	16.3	17
Montana	7.4	19	7.1	36	—	—
Nebraska	7.7	23	7.2	39	—	—
Nevada	6.5	7	6.2	10	—	—
New Hampshire	6.2	3	6.1	9	—	—
New Jersey	7.7	23	5.8	4	16.3	17
New Mexico	8.3	34	7.9	47	—	—
New York	7.8	26	6.0	6	14.4	7
North Carolina	10.0	46	7.5	43	16.6	21
North Dakota	7.2	18	6.5	19	—	—
Ohio	8.7	38	7.2	39	17.7	22
Oklahoma	8.5	36	8.3	49	11.3	2
Oregon	7.1	16	6.9	31	—	—
Pennsylvania	8.2	33	6.4	15	18.6	25
Rhode Island	5.0	1	4.1	1	—	—
South Carolina	9.3	43	6.6	24	14.1	6
South Dakota	9.6	45	7.6	44	—	—
Tennessee	8.9	40	6.3	13	18.0	23
Texas	7.1	16	6.4	15	12.6	3
Utah	6.2	3	5.8	4	—	—
Vermont	7.5	20	7.6	44	—	—
Virginia	8.3	34	6.4	15	15.1	12
Washington	6.2	3	6.0	6	14.7	8
West Virginia	6.7	8	6.6	24	—	—
Wisconsin	7.9	29	6.5	19	20.2	30
Wyoming	6.7	8	6.6	24	—	—
United States	8.0		6.6		15.8	

*Infant deaths per 1,000 live births.
— Number too small to calculate a reliable rate.

Source: U.S. Department of Health and Human Services, National Center for Health Statistics. Ranks calculated by Children's Defense Fund.

TABLE B6.

Health Insurance Coverage and Immunization Status of Children

	Children Lacking Insurance Throughout the Year, 1993–1995*			Percent of 19- to 35-Month-Old Children Fully Immunized,** July 1994–June 1995	
	Number	Percent	Rank	Percent	Rank
Alabama	171,900	16.0%	40	76%	22
Alaska	17,830	9.4	10	68	43
Arizona	231,593	20.2	48	71	32
Arkansas	121,888	19.0	46	68	43
California	1,587,464	18.3	44	69	39
Colorado	115,216	12.0	30	70	36
Connecticut	77,309	9.8	13	84	3
Delaware	21,030	11.9	29	77	18
District of Columbia	18,654	16.2	41	62	50
Florida	563,866	17.1	42	78	13
Georgia	292,090	15.5	39	74	26
Hawaii	24,288	8.0	4	78	13
Idaho	46,096	13.6	36	67	47
Illinois	307,339	9.9	15	72	30
Indiana	161,420	10.9	20	71	32
Iowa	76,284	10.5	18	81	8
Kansas	72,174	10.5	18	75	23
Kentucky	126,463	13.0	34	83	4
Louisiana	245,939	19.9	47	70	36
Maine	37,020	12.1	31	82	6
Maryland	146,606	11.6	25	74	26
Massachusetts	127,998	9.0	7	83	4
Michigan	207,867	8.3	5	61	51
Minnesota	82,470	6.7	1	78	13
Mississippi	133,944	17.7	43	81	8
Missouri	152,993	11.2	22	70	36
Montana	26,645	11.4	23	68	43
Nebraska	39,886	9.1	8	71	32
Nevada	70,717	18.7	45	64	49
New Hampshire	28,967	9.9	15	85	2
New Jersey	221,231	11.4	23	73	28
New Mexico	121,443	24.7	51	71	32
New York	557,155	12.4	32	77	18
North Carolina	228,986	13.0	34	79	12
North Dakota	14,826	8.7	6	81	8
Ohio	267,221	9.4	10	75	23
Oklahoma	196,801	22.6	49	69	39
Oregon	92,407	11.8	27	68	43
Pennsylvania	289,422	10.0	17	77	18
Rhode Island	25,743	10.9	20	82	6
South Carolina	137,652	14.6	38	80	11
South Dakota	19,481	9.4	10	78	13
Tennessee	152,916	11.8	27	72	30
Texas	1,203,481	22.7	50	69	39
Utah	65,627	9.8	13	69	39
Vermont	10,987	7.5	3	87	1
Virginia	185,006	11.6	25	78	13
Washington	130,571	9.3	9	73	28
West Virginia	53,469	12.5	33	67	47
Wisconsin	91,571	6.8	2	75	23
Wyoming	19,280	14.1	37	77	18
United States	9,795,000	13.8%		73%	

*Averages of the number and percent of uninsured persons younger than 18 from 1993 through 1995 for states, and 1995 for the U.S.
**Four doses of diphtheria-pertussis-tetanus vaccine, three doses of polio vaccine, one dose of measles-mumps-rubella vaccine, and three doses of H. flu type b vaccine. Not wholly comparable to previous periods when fewer vaccines constituted full immunization.

Source: U.S. Department of Commerce, Bureau of the Census; and U.S. Department of Health and Human Services, Centers for Disease Control and Prevention. Calculations by Children's Defense Fund.

TABLE B7.

Head Start Enrollment, by Race/Ethnicity, 1996

	Number	Percentage of children enrolled, by racial/ethnic group				
		White	Black	Hispanic	Asian, Pacific Islander	Native American
Alabama	15,897	22%	76%	2%	0%	0%
Alaska	3,179	21	5	4	2	68
Arizona	17,063	18	6	40	1	36
Arkansas	10,978	50	45	4	0	0
California	95,172	17	16	59	7	1
Colorado	9,786	34	10	51	2	3
Connecticut	6,375	22	45	31	1	0
Delaware	2,030	20	65	14	0	0
District of Columbia	3,266	0	85	13	1	0
Florida	29,885	18	62	19	1	0
Georgia	20,942	21	73	5	1	0
Hawaii	2,615	17	6	7	70	0
Idaho	3,405	50	1	40	1	8
Illinois	35,641	26	55	17	1	0
Indiana	13,492	64	31	5	0	0
Iowa	6,942	78	13	6	2	1
Kansas	6,582	52	28	15	2	3
Kentucky	15,988	78	20	1	1	0
Louisiana	20,750	17	82	1	1	0
Maine	4,121	92	2	3	1	3
Maryland	10,733	20	70	8	2	0
Massachusetts	12,593	42	22	29	6	1
Michigan	36,849	49	40	8	1	2
Minnesota	14,928	50	14	19	8	9
Mississippi	22,212	12	86	0	1	1
Missouri	16,887	58	39	2	1	0
Montana	4,338	50	1	3	1	45
Nebraska	4,464	56	17	17	1	8
Nevada	2,619	27	32	28	1	11
New Hampshire	1,264	91	4	4	1	1
New Jersey	14,157	14	56	29	1	0
New Mexico	7,964	17	3	60	1	20
New York	46,609	30	36	31	3	1
North Carolina	17,792	25	65	7	1	3
North Dakota	2,957	55	2	2	1	40
Ohio	50,919	52	44	3	1	0
Oklahoma	16,019	47	22	6	1	24
Oregon	8,836	50	6	36	2	6
Pennsylvania	29,965	49	40	10	1	0
Rhode Island	2,779	52	22	19	4	2
South Carolina	11,199	8	87	3	0	3
South Dakota	4,057	42	2	2	1	53
Tennessee	15,337	55	42	2	1	0
Texas	58,199	14	31	54	1	0
Utah	5,330	61	2	26	3	7
Vermont	1,440	94	1	1	2	1
Virginia	14,516	35	47	15	3	0
Washington	14,578	36	9	39	7	8
West Virginia	7,507	89	11	0	0	0
Wisconsin	15,628	46	31	9	7	7
Wyoming	1,729	61	3	20	1	14
United States	798,513	32%	36%	25%	3%	4%

Source: U.S. Department of Health and Human Services, Administration for Children and Families.

TABLE B8.

Maximum Number of Children Allowed per Caretaker and Maximum Group Size in Child Care Centers, 1996

	Children per Caretaker			Group Size		
	9 Months	27 Months	4 Years	9 Months	27 Months	4 Years
Alabama	6:1	8:1	20:1	6	8	20
Alaska	5:1	6:1	10:1	NR	NR	NR
Arizona	5:1/11:2	8:1	15:1	NR	NR	NR
Arkansas	6:1	12:1	15:1	NR	NR	NR
California	4:1	12:1/15:2	12:1/15:2	NR	NR	NR
Colorado	5:1	7:1	12:1	10	14	24
Connecticut	4:1	4:1	10:1	8	8	20
Delaware	4:1	10:1	15:1	NR	NR	NR
District of Columbia	4:1	4:1	10:1	8	8	20
Florida	4:1	11:1	20:1	NR	NR	NR
Georgia	6:1	10:1	18:1	12	20	36
Hawaii	4:1	8:1	16:1	8	NR	NR
Idaho	12:1	12:1	12:1	NR	NR	NR
Illinois	4:1	8:1	10:1	12	16	20
Indiana	5:1	5:1	12:1	10	15	NR
Iowa	4:1	6:1	12:1	NR	NR	NR
Kansas	3:1	7:1	12:1	9	14	24
Kentucky	5:1	10:1	14:1	10	20	28
Louisiana	6:1	12:1	16:1	NR	NR	NR
Maine	4:1	5:1	10:1	12	15	30
Maryland	3:1	6:1	10:1	6	12	20
Massachusetts	3:1/7:2	4:1/9:2	10:1	7	9	20
Michigan	4:1	4:1	12:1	NR	NR	NR
Minnesota	4:1	7:1	10:1	8	14	20
Mississippi	5:1	12:1	16:1	10	14	16
Missouri	4:1	8:1	10:1	8	16	NR
Montana	4:1	8:1	10:1	NR	NR	NR
Nebraska	4:1	6:1	12:1	NR	NR	NR
Nevada	6:1	10:1	13:1	NR	NR	NR
New Hampshire	4:1	6:1	12:1	12	18	24
New Jersey	4:1	7:1	15:1	20	20	20
New Mexico	6:1	10:1	12:1	NR	NR	NR
New York	4:1	5:1	8:1	8	10	16
North Carolina	5:1	10:1	20:1	10	20	25
North Dakota	4:1	5:1	10:1	NR	NR	NR
Ohio	5:1	7:1	12:1	12	14	28
Oklahoma	4:1	8:1	15:1	8	16	30
Oregon	4:1	4:1	10:1	8	8	20
Pennsylvania	4:1	6:1	10:1	8	12	20
Rhode Island	4:1	6:1	10:1	8	12	20
South Carolina	6:1	10:1	18:1	NR	NR	NR
South Dakota	5:1	5:1	10:1	20	20	20
Tennessee	5:1	8:1	15:1	10	16	20
Texas	5:1/12:2	13:1	20:1	5/12	35	35
Utah	4:1	7:1	15:1	8	25	25
Vermont	4:1	5:1	10:1	8	10	20
Virginia	4:1	8:1	16:1	NR	NR	NR
Washington	4:1	7:1	10:1	8	14	20
West Virginia	4:1	8:1	12:1	NR	NR	NR
Wisconsin	4:1	6:1	13:1	8	12	24
Wyoming	5:1	8:1	15:1	NR	NR	NR

NR Not regulated.

Source: The Center for Career Development in Early Care and Education, Wheelock College, Boston.

TABLE B9.

Number of Children Reported Abused or Neglected, and Distribution by Race and Ethnicity, 1994

	Total Number Reported	Total, Race/ Ethnicity Reported	White	Black	Hispanic	Native American	Asian, Pacific Islander	Other	Race/ Ethnicity Unknown
Alabama	40,164	21,584	12,417	8,930	80	29	54	0	74
Alaska	10,071	6,819	3,085	601	169	2,381	84	81	418
Arizona	48,722	29,531	17,586	1,978	6,887	1,022	148	242	1,668
Arkansas	18,429	7,816	5,416	2,189	89	14	0	80	28
California	449,177	62,343	29,891	7,140	20,342	304	1,901	867	1,898
Colorado	43,919	7,815	4,774	882	1,727	98	102	0	232
Connecticut	37,043	27,618	12,881	6,397	4,946	10	135	127	3,122
Delaware	9,441	2,542	1,283	1,046	116	7	3	37	50
District of Columbia	13,369	n/a	n/a	n/a	n/a	n/a	n/a	n/a	n/a
Florida	164,945	69,359	45,306	23,499	0	53	233	0	268
Georgia	89,958	63,721	32,764	26,263	986	57	199	1,191	2,261
Hawaii	5,944	2,380	337	39	28	24	1,107	585	260
Idaho	34,313	9,461	5,776	49	639	99	21	99	2,778
Illinois	140,651	53,056	21,926	26,216	3,439	53	140	815	467
Indiana	62,553	25,343	19,822	4,096	468	17	20	659	261
Iowa	31,240	9,172	7,592	953	179	124	61	16	247
Kansas	33,928	33,928	24,838	5,932	1,839	347	196	426	350
Kentucky	59,540	24,877	20,935	3,060	80	12	37	634	119
Louisiana	44,901	15,015	6,169	8,493	86	4	26	132	105
Maine	8,902	4,769	n/a	n/a	n/a	n/a	n/a	n/a	4,769
Maryland	40,934	n/a	n/a	n/a	n/a	n/a	n/a	n/a	n/a
Massachusetts	56,178	26,325	14,422	5,096	4,473	32	457	974	871
Michigan	136,989	21,951	12,554	8,187	493	118	84	0	515
Minnesota	26,483	9,551	5,857	2,133	588	738	171	0	64
Mississippi	27,123	7,730	2,845	4,159	23	16	11	22	654
Missouri	86,007	21,567	15,536	5,734	103	43	49	88	14
Montana	13,528	4,194	2,701	21	78	608	9	777	0
Nebraska	17,508	4,514	3,302	617	274	206	28	0	87
Nevada	21,060	8,037	5,745	1,193	797	104	132	62	4
New Hampshire	9,666	1,043	572	6	0	0	6	0	459
New Jersey	65,954	9,519	2,867	4,428	1,395	14	91	15	709
New Mexico	24,933	7,356	2,320	237	3,001	657	30	0	1,111
New York	210,997	54,993	23,957	19,219	8,122	180	253	2,244	1,018
North Carolina	95,144	29,479	15,163	12,609	473	734	127	0	373
North Dakota	7,753	3,617	2,722	56	66	686	16	42	29
Ohio	156,635	52,744	32,415	14,134	761	56	87	2,278	3,013
Oklahoma	34,846	10,891	7,319	1,733	333	1,468	22	15	1
Oregon	41,769	7,946	6,122	425	400	212	60	0	727
Pennsylvania	23,722	n/a	n/a	n/a	n/a	n/a	n/a	n/a	n/a
Rhode Island	14,303	3,207	1,977	491	480	22	77	95	65
South Carolina	40,461	11,628	4,941	6,481	21	13	11	161	0
South Dakota	10,156	1,923	825	0	0	1,022	0	42	34
Tennessee	34,714	12,175	7,623	4,152	62	4	18	146	170
Texas	173,644	55,266	22,980	13,533	17,734	98	321	600	0
Utah	29,112	10,430	8,421	238	850	424	128	0	369
Vermont	3,025	1,234	1,204	14	1	3	7	2	3
Virginia	56,331	10,264	5,067	4,404	354	8	111	320	0
Washington	57,100	44,197	29,811	3,961	3,508	2,488	1,085	230	3,114
West Virginia	19,544	n/a	n/a	n/a	n/a	n/a	n/a	n/a	n/a
Wisconsin	47,561	18,185	11,754	4,448	671	708	284	0	320
Wyoming	5,080	n/a	n/a	n/a	n/a	n/a	n/a	n/a	n/a
United States	2,935,470	928,817	523,820	245,472	87,161	15,317	8,142	14,104	34,801

n/a Data not available.

Source: U.S. Department of Health and Human Services, National Center on Child Abuse and Neglect.

TABLE B10.

Children Under 18 in Foster Care,
FY 1990–FY 1994

	Last Day FY 1990	Last Day FY 1991	Last Day FY 1992	Last Day FY 1993	Last Day FY 1994	Percent Change FY90–94
Alabama	4,420	4,383	4,133	3,938	3,788	−14.3%
Alaska	3,852	1,942	1,496	2,029	1,876	−51.3
Arizona	3,379	3,618	3,909	4,107	4,271	26.4
Arkansas	1,351	1,326	1,981	2,296	2,196	62.5
California	79,482	80,880	83,849	88,262	93,321	17.4
Colorado	3,892	5,519	4,390	5,700	5,957	53.1
Connecticut	4,121	4,202	4,252	4,557	4,648	12.8
Delaware	663	655	638	707	746	12.5
District of Columbia	2,313	—	2,152	2,145	1,981	−14.4
Florida	10,664	10,235	9,928	9,568	9,284	−12.9
Georgia	15,179	15,500	16,999	17,277	17,239	13.6
Hawaii	1,659	1,600	1,214	1,574	1,818	9.6
Idaho	548	877	1,235	1,342	906	65.3
Illinois	20,753	23,776	29,542	33,815	41,161	98.3
Indiana	7,492	8,126	8,455	8,669	9,883	31.9
Iowa	3,425	4,609	3,606	3,411	3,526	2.9
Kansas	3,976	7,112	7,838	4,593	4,501	13.2
Kentucky	3,810	6,422	6,966	3,363	3,567	−6.4
Louisiana	5,379	5,799	5,722	5,607	5,831	8.4
Maine	1,745	1,814	1,944	2,150	2,236	28.1
Maryland	6,473	4,859	5,816	6,107	6,936	7.2
Massachusetts	11,856	13,232	13,147	13,382	13,574	14.5
Michigan	9,000	11,282	11,121	10,382	10,606	17.8
Minnesota	7,310	7,898	7,895	9,700	10,379	42.0
Mississippi	2,832	2,830	3,169	3,293	3,425	20.9
Missouri	8,241	7,143	8,171	8,625	8,873	7.7
Montana	1,224	1,494	1,691	1,447	1,414	15.5
Nebraska	2,543	2,660	2,985	3,222	3,274	28.7
Nevada	2,566	1,563	1,664	2,831	2,440	−4.9
New Hampshire	1,505	2,095	2,630	2,509	1,975	31.2
New Jersey	8,879	8,451	8,024	7,673	7,771	−12.5
New Mexico	2,042	2,304	2,118	2,097	2,174	6.5
New York	63,371	65,171	62,705	59,658	58,658	−7.4
North Carolina	7,170	9,619	10,275	11,024	11,859	65.4
North Dakota	393	695	759	805	875	122.6
Ohio	18,062	17,298	17,099	15,922	15,922	−11.8
Oklahoma	3,435	3,803	2,892	2,953	6,707	95.3
Oregon	4,261	3,996	4,031	4,119	4,599	7.9
Pennsylvania	16,665	17,508	18,491	18,976	19,735	18.4
Rhode Island	2,680	3,311	2,755	2,830	3,139	17.1
South Carolina	3,286	3,698	5,066	4,656	4,761	44.9
South Dakota	567	613	674	710	631	11.3
Tennessee	4,971	5,217	5,312	5,835	6,186	24.4
Texas	6,698	7,200	9,965	10,880	11,315	68.9
Utah	1,174	1,405	895	1,465	1,622	38.2
Vermont	1,063	1,088	1,162	1,236	1,336	25.7
Virginia	6,217	6,590	6,305	6,229	6,429	3.4
Washington	13,302	13,956	11,327	8,394	9,189	−30.9
West Virginia	1,997	1,997	2,315	2,483	2,483	24.3
Wisconsin	6,037	6,403	6,812	7,045	8,058	33.5
Wyoming	484	605	907	620	957	97.7
United States	404,407	424,379	438,427	442,218	466,038	15.2%

Source: American Public Welfare Association.

TABLE B11.

Participants in Federal Education and Disability Programs

	Title I 1993–1994	Bilingual/ESL 1994–1995	IDEA and Chapter 1 Disabled, 1994–1995				SSI Blind and Disabled December 1994
			Total	3–5	6–17	18–21	
Alabama	126,446	3,502	99,171	8,498	85,525	5,148	4,779
Alaska	9,225	29,929	17,552	2,068	14,884	600	272
Arizona	105,703	98,128	72,462	7,277	62,359	2,826	2,454
Arkansas	90,740	4,405	52,637	6,901	43,505	2,231	3,274
California	1,415,387	1,262,982	544,423	52,023	471,825	20,575	16,212
Colorado	45,918	26,765	68,158	6,760	58,647	2,751	2,489
Connecticut	51,527	20,392	73,798	6,963	63,391	3,444	1,266
Delaware	10,288	1,799	15,424	2,010	12,808	606	516
District of Columbia	9,781	5,221	6,627	338	5,794	495	846
Florida	212,519	153,841	294,608	25,177	258,854	10,577	13,442
Georgia	160,560	12,865	129,222	12,791	111,972	4,459	5,319
Hawaii	15,138	12,216	15,137	1,199	13,441	497	185
Idaho	26,975	8,959	22,868	2,980	19,176	712	801
Illinois	201,760	107,084	251,434	25,018	215,938	10,478	10,896
Indiana	91,487	6,293	128,576	11,065	111,550	5,961	3,936
Iowa	32,397	5,807	64,028	5,673	55,352	3,003	1,585
Kansas	39,967	10,148	51,661	5,856	43,821	1,984	2,223
Kentucky	115,136	2,161	80,759	14,009	63,606	3,144	4,891
Louisiana	120,009	6,566	88,711	9,658	74,677	4,376	7,268
Maine	26,237	2,430	30,613	3,268	26,036	1,309	500
Maryland	67,572	14,687	96,771	9,052	84,051	3,668	2,924
Massachusetts	88,270	44,476	156,670	14,267	134,443	7,960	3,734
Michigan	176,450	47,123	182,903	17,672	156,430	8,801	9,850
Minnesota	87,525	21,738	93,975	10,758	79,735	3,482	3,105
Mississippi	150,933	2,748	65,546	6,451	56,398	2,697	4,438
Missouri	114,461	5,442	116,826	7,975	104,095	4,756	3,958
Montana	20,200	8,599	17,679	1,635	15,337	707	543
Nebraska	33,497	4,017	38,056	3,313	33,304	1,439	861
Nevada	13,456	23,390	26,363	2,900	22,597	866	712
New Hampshire	13,852	1,084	23,754	1,996	20,628	1,130	382
New Jersey	164,312	52,081	191,912	15,942	167,549	8,421	4,711
New Mexico	64,030	84,457	45,364	4,116	39,594	1,654	1,284
New York	441,122	236,356	374,361	45,009	308,722	20,630	16,503
North Carolina	110,736	14,901	139,560	15,141	120,021	4,398	5,869
North Dakota	12,676	8,531	12,176	1,119	10,432	625	289
Ohio	203,097	12,243	223,640	18,193	194,069	11,378	14,125
Oklahoma	66,992	31,562	70,809	4,970	62,740	3,099	2,011
Oregon	56,840	25,701	66,944	5,648	58,610	2,686	1,488
Pennsylvania	266,529	19,889	207,436	19,715	177,291	10,430	9,786
Rhode Island	14,909	9,093	23,693	2,131	20,509	1,053	618
South Carolina	60,121	1,891	82,626	9,904	69,765	2,957	3,608
South Dakota	14,433	8,517	15,755	2,227	12,908	620	512
Tennessee	124,352	4,119	123,753	9,825	107,917	6,011	4,661
Texas	663,826	457,437	420,540	30,647	368,556	21,337	9,881
Utah	41,973	21,360	51,218	4,568	45,009	1,641	1,164
Vermont	11,637	869	10,720	1,184	9,039	497	283
Virginia	74,328	n/a	136,166	12,746	117,752	5,668	5,338
Washington	73,375	51,598	104,483	12,830	87,370	4,283	3,110
West Virginia	36,724	n/a	45,318	4,461	38,666	2,191	1,774
Wisconsin	72,042	20,787	102,237	13,072	84,595	4,570	4,641
Wyoming	7,150	1,853	12,150	1,495	10,193	462	293
United States	6,255,047	3,018,042	5,387,273	520,494	4,631,486	235,293	205,610

n/a Data not available.

Source: U.S. Department of Education and Social Security Administration.

TABLE B12.

Adolescent Childbearing in the States, 1980, 1990, and 1994

	1980 Teen Birth Rate*	1990 Teen Birth Rate*	Percent Change, 1980–1990	Percent of All Births That Were to Teens, 1994	Percent of Teen Births That Were to Unmarried Teens, 1994
Alabama	68.3	71.3	4.4%	18.6%	70.0%
Alaska	64.4	65.4	1.6	11.5	75.9
Arizona	65.5	75.9	15.9	15.3	79.8
Arkansas	74.5	80.1	7.5	20.1	64.7
California	53.3	71.5	34.1	12.3	70.5
Colorado	49.9	54.9	10.0	12.3	73.1
Connecticut	30.5	39.2	28.5	8.5	88.0
Delaware	51.2	55.0	7.4	13.2	90.2
District of Columbia	62.4	95.8	53.5	16.4	96.8
Florida	58.5	69.5	18.8	13.7	78.5
Georgia	71.9	75.9	5.6	16.2	75.1
Hawaii	50.7	61.7	21.7	10.5	80.3
Idaho	59.5	50.7	–14.8	13.1	54.8
Illinois	55.8	63.3	13.4	13.0	83.7
Indiana	57.5	58.7	2.1	14.5	77.9
Iowa	43.0	40.7	–5.3	10.9	79.6
Kansas	56.8	56.4	–0.7	12.9	71.4
Kentucky	72.3	67.7	–6.4	17.2	59.8
Louisiana	76.0	74.4	–2.1	19.2	81.7
Maine	47.4	43.3	–8.6	10.2	81.1
Maryland	43.4	53.7	23.7	10.3	88.2
Massachusetts	28.1	35.7	27.0	7.8	89.6
Michigan	45.0	59.3	31.8	12.6	87.3
Minnesota	35.4	36.5	3.1	8.5	85.4
Mississippi	83.7	81.0	–3.2	22.1	79.7
Missouri	57.8	63.0	9.0	14.7	76.3
Montana	48.5	48.7	0.4	12.1	71.3
Nebraska	45.1	42.5	–5.8	11.0	79.6
Nevada	58.5	74.2	26.8	13.3	69.7
New Hampshire	33.6	33.2	–1.2	7.0	82.9
New Jersey	35.2	40.9	16.2	8.2	88.4
New Mexico	71.8	78.4	9.2	18.0	80.5
New York	34.8	44.1	26.7	9.5	85.6
North Carolina	57.5	68.0	18.3	15.5	74.6
North Dakota	41.7	35.6	–14.6	9.4	77.2
Ohio	52.5	58.1	10.7	13.7	82.0
Oklahoma	74.6	67.2	–9.9	17.1	62.7
Oregon	50.9	54.9	7.9	12.8	74.5
Pennsylvania	40.5	45.3	11.9	10.8	88.1
Rhode Island	33.0	44.6	35.2	10.6	89.0
South Carolina	64.8	71.5	10.3	17.0	78.8
South Dakota	52.6	46.9	–10.8	11.4	78.1
Tennessee	64.1	72.6	13.3	17.4	68.4
Texas	74.3	75.6	1.7	16.5	63.2
Utah	65.2	48.7	–25.3	10.7	57.2
Vermont	39.5	34.3	–13.2	8.5	80.3
Virginia	48.3	53.3	10.4	11.3	75.9
Washington	46.7	53.5	14.6	11.1	73.8
West Virginia	67.8	57.4	–15.3	17.4	64.0
Wisconsin	39.5	42.8	8.4	10.3	83.9
Wyoming	78.7	56.5	–28.2	14.5	66.5
United States	53.0	59.9	13.0%	13.1%	75.9%

*Births per 1,000 young women ages 15–19.
Note: Years shown are most recent years for which reliable data are available.

Source: U.S. Department of Health and Human Services, National Center for Health Statistics; and U.S. Department of Commerce, Bureau of the Census. Calculations by Children's Defense Fund.

TABLE B13.

Firearm Deaths Among Children Ages 0–19, by Cause, 1993

	Total Firearm Deaths	Homicide Deaths	Suicide Deaths	Accident Deaths	Intent Unknown
Alabama	135	71	34	26	4
Alaska	22	3	16	3	0
Arizona	127	53	50	19	5
Arkansas	69	39	24	5	1
California	904	711	141	44	8
Colorado	65	28	28	7	2
Connecticut	47	39	6	2	0
Delaware	5	3	2	0	0
District of Columbia	100	98	1	1	0
Florida	237	154	64	17	2
Georgia	165	92	41	25	7
Hawaii	3	0	1	1	1
Idaho	21	4	12	5	0
Illinois	363	297	45	15	6
Indiana	95	44	31	18	2
Iowa	26	8	15	3	0
Kansas	61	32	22	5	2
Kentucky	56	20	17	18	1
Louisiana	232	166	46	18	2
Maine	10	2	7	1	0
Maryland	110	91	15	1	3
Massachusetts	44	32	10	0	2
Michigan	235	158	58	15	4
Minnesota	39	22	15	2	0
Mississippi	106	52	31	22	1
Missouri	177	127	31	17	2
Montana	30	6	18	5	1
Nebraska	17	9	5	3	0
Nevada	33	13	13	4	3
New Hampshire	8	2	6	0	0
New Jersey	60	39	18	2	1
New Mexico	40	18	17	4	1
New York	344	288	44	8	4
North Carolina	161	93	38	30	0
North Dakota	7	2	4	0	1
Ohio	175	98	50	25	2
Oklahoma	82	34	35	9	4
Oregon	45	16	20	8	1
Pennsylvania	174	107	53	11	3
Rhode Island	10	7	3	0	0
South Carolina	89	47	28	12	2
South Dakota	17	5	10	1	1
Tennessee	114	48	43	23	0
Texas	515	317	125	53	20
Utah	37	7	26	4	0
Vermont	8	0	7	1	0
Virginia	122	64	42	16	0
Washington	82	45	25	8	4
West Virginia	31	13	15	2	1
Wisconsin	82	37	41	4	0
Wyoming	14	0	11	3	0
United States	5,751	3,661	1,460	526	104

Source: U.S. Department of Health and Human Services, National Center for Health Statistics, computed by the Office of Analysis, Epidemiology and Health Promotion from data compiled by the Division of Vital Statistics.

TABLE B14.

Fair Market Rent* vs. the Minimum Wage, 1997

	Lowest Monthly Rent	Hourly Minimum Wage**	Lowest Rent As % of Minimum Wage	Rank
Alabama	$348	$4.75	43.9%	1
Alaska	750	5.25	85.7	50
Arizona	545	4.75	68.8	41
Arkansas	380	4.75	53.7	20
California	472	4.75	59.6	28
Colorado	485	4.75	61.2	36
Connecticut	675	4.77	84.9	49
Delaware	591	5.00	70.9	42
District of Columbia	794	5.75	82.9	48
Florida	477	4.75	60.2	32
Georgia	412	4.75	52.0	13
Hawaii	982	5.25	112.2	51
Idaho	404	4.75	51.0	10
Illinois	428	4.75	54.0	21
Indiana	396	4.75	50.0	7
Iowa	416	4.75	52.5	16
Kansas	478	4.75	60.4	33
Kentucky	383	4.75	48.4	6
Louisiana	380	4.75	48.0	4
Maine	484	4.75	61.1	35
Maryland	472	4.75	59.6	28
Massachusetts	568	5.25	64.9	39
Michigan	474	4.75	59.8	30
Minnesota	440	4.75	55.6	22
Mississippi	377	4.75	47.6	3
Missouri	376	4.75	47.5	2
Montana	463	4.75	58.5	26
Nebraska	493	4.75	62.2	37
Nevada	630	4.75	79.5	47
New Hampshire	627	4.75	79.2	46
New Jersey	660	5.05	78.4	45
New Mexico	418	4.75	52.8	17
New York	465	4.75	58.7	27
North Carolina	410	4.75	51.8	12
North Dakota	475	4.75	60.0	31
Ohio	402	4.75	50.8	8
Oklahoma	381	4.75	48.1	5
Oregon	554	5.50	60.4	33
Pennsylvania	423	4.75	53.4	18
Rhode Island	647	5.15	75.4	43
South Carolina	414	4.75	52.3	14
South Dakota	521	4.75	65.8	40
Tennessee	423	4.75	53.4	18
Texas	406	4.75	51.3	11
Utah	444	4.75	56.1	25
Vermont	642	5.00	77.1	44
Virginia	415	4.75	52.4	15
Washington	527	4.90	64.5	38
West Virginia	402	4.75	50.8	8
Wisconsin	440	4.75	55.6	22
Wyoming	442	4.75	55.8	24

*HUD Fair Market Rent for a two-bedroom apartment is for the metropolitan county with the lowest FMR in the state.
**Minimum wage as of January 1, 1997; the federal minimum wage will be raised to $5.15 on September 1, 1997.

Source: U.S. Department of Housing and Urban Development and U.S. Department of Labor. Calculations by Children's Defense Fund.

TABLE B15.

Number of Children Participating in Food Stamps and Child Nutrition Programs, FY 1996

	Food Stamps*	WIC Women	WIC Infants	WIC Children	WIC Total	School Lunch	School Breakfast	Child/ Adult Care	Summer Food
Alabama	281,000	26,493	35,021	56,650	118,163	547,349	139,551	34,696	40,256
Alaska	24,000	5,119	4,939	12,352	22,410	46,967	7,690	7,490	345
Arizona	284,000	34,470	36,113	70,899	141,482	404,687	124,563	39,504	31,909
Arkansas	133,000	23,354	23,086	44,222	90,662	313,142	113,252	20,289	10,290
California	2,035,000	281,534	268,908	591,155	1,141,598	2,402,411	765,375	256,304	186,275
Colorado	126,000	17,632	17,276	35,616	70,524	307,121	47,736	37,286	15,001
Connecticut	128,000	10,941	14,362	37,218	62,520	233,884	44,571	20,333	22,989
Delaware	28,000	3,195	4,346	8,336	15,877	66,700	15,388	11,855	6,968
District of Columbia	52,000	3,447	4,999	7,758	16,203	49,657	16,517	4,301	19,805
Florida	720,000	70,569	90,516	171,049	332,134	1,221,786	354,730	73,096	194,193
Georgia	421,000	52,051	57,116	114,580	223,746	1,009,743	329,750	77,031	93,769
Hawaii	61,000	6,041	7,215	14,210	27,466	143,461	36,031	8,590	3,206
Idaho	41,000	6,962	7,441	16,682	31,085	140,027	22,986	6,264	2,292
Illinois	581,000	48,575	72,618	122,940	244,133	972,984	168,285	74,944	115,988
Indiana	219,000	32,956	36,869	62,867	132,691	597,185	96,951	40,326	11,680
Iowa	93,000	14,243	13,875	37,902	66,020	378,310	51,209	27,979	6,755
Kansas	99,000	12,265	12,973	28,745	53,983	304,860	62,759	54,297	2,216
Kentucky	224,000	27,548	29,127	62,690	119,365	505,787	167,995	38,064	32,506
Louisiana	384,000	34,789	40,052	64,665	139,506	661,962	229,501	56,763	66,712
Maine	53,000	5,680	5,626	15,009	26,315	104,087	21,640	14,015	5,546
Maryland	206,000	20,887	25,279	41,827	87,993	372,230	71,808	52,325	32,159
Massachusetts	232,000	25,666	27,005	63,345	116,016	476,308	92,143	49,700	34,627
Michigan	490,000	46,175	51,480	114,348	212,003	757,860	155,805	70,968	44,953
Minnesota	163,000	19,570	21,107	53,507	94,184	531,563	68,561	94,000	19,077
Mississippi	250,000	21,464	29,979	51,088	102,532	403,128	163,870	25,851	33,977
Missouri	292,000	31,555	32,879	64,812	129,245	560,767	131,425	41,388	28,319
Montana	35,000	4,856	4,312	12,986	22,155	85,115	13,649	12,855	4,013
Nebraska	54,000	7,920	9,144	19,072	36,136	207,835	22,890	38,813	10,047
Nevada	56,000	9,138	9,179	17,990	36,307	99,176	26,300	4,740	3,973
New Hampshire	28,000	4,075	4,661	10,606	19,342	93,828	14,417	7,127	2,503
New Jersey	284,000	31,857	33,997	72,402	138,256	531,003	71,759	43,623	63,498
New Mexico	126,000	12,423	12,463	31,258	56,144	189,473	69,747	41,903	59,282
New York	950,000	96,448	117,167	253,057	466,672	1,670,309	423,684	156,438	338,750
North Carolina	301,000	46,893	50,263	91,684	188,840	772,149	225,745	100,894	39,238
North Dakota	19,000	3,709	3,666	10,110	17,484	86,348	10,853	18,405	2,692
Ohio	575,000	58,155	76,129	123,976	258,260	965,987	163,055	82,722	38,756
Oklahoma	186,000	24,174	26,407	52,792	103,373	367,322	120,165	41,529	12,877
Oregon	140,000	21,366	16,198	48,519	86,083	253,105	63,418	34,660	12,759
Pennsylvania	536,000	53,069	57,845	151,545	262,460	999,933	152,619	63,283	114,946
Rhode Island	50,000	4,465	5,166	12,726	22,357	57,421	6,899	6,743	10,372
South Carolina	199,000	29,464	23,076	62,129	123,669	452,942	154,300	25,097	73,030
South Dakota	28,000	4,931	5,095	12,411	22,437	105,719	14,739	11,749	5,509
Tennessee	315,000	35,366	52,912	55,896	144,174	603,829	174,267	36,469	37,080
Texas	1,406,000	155,565	163,642	321,921	641,128	2,218,690	739,380	154,403	104,113
Utah	65,000	14,241	13,554	27,014	54,809	249,933	24,853	39,919	19,269
Vermont	29,000	3,610	2,880	9,571	16,061	50,256	11,325	8,924	2,568
Virginia	277,000	27,600	30,062	69,211	126,873	626,480	157,414	41,677	37,850
Washington	249,000	29,695	33,287	66,307	129,289	433,062	97,939	53,065	25,945
West Virginia	123,000	12,317	12,536	29,165	54,018	201,397	81,200	10,219	13,445
Wisconsin	186,000	23,003	24,227	62,457	109,686	509,348	38,557	50,318	22,347
Wyoming	19,000	2,952	2,636	6,377	11,965	56,506	7,386	8,116	645
United States	13,859,000	1,600,475	1,769,706	3,595,649	6,965,830	25,401,131	6,386,654	2,331,343	2,117,320

Note: These are averages of participation each month that the program is operating. The school lunch numbers include all schools and children receiving a federal subsidy for lunch, including children receiving free and reduced-price lunches.

*State enrollments are rounded to the nearest 1,000; the U.S. total may not be the same as the sum of the state enrollments because of this rounding.

Source: U.S. Department of Agriculture, Food and Consumer Service.

Supplementary Tables

TABLE C1.

**Percent of Births with Selected Characteristics,
by Race and Hispanic Origin of Mother, 1994**

	All Races	White	Black	Native American	Asian, Pacific Islander	Hispanic
Early prenatal care*	80.2	82.8	68.3	65.2	79.9	68.9
Late or no prenatal care**	4.4	3.6	8.2	9.8	4.1	7.6
Low birthweight***	7.3	6.1	13.2	6.4	6.8	6.2
Very low birthweight****	1.3	1.0	3.0	1.1	0.9	1.1
Births to teens	13.1	11.3	23.2	21.0	5.7	17.8
Births to unmarried women	32.6	25.4	70.4	57.0	16.2	43.1
Births to mothers who have not completed high school	22.9	21.7	29.3	34.0	17.4	52.7

*Prenatal care begun in the first three months of pregnancy.
**Prenatal care begun in the last three months of pregnancy, or not at all.
***Less than 2,500 grams (5 lbs., 8 oz.).
****Less than 1,500 grams (3 lbs., 5 oz.).

Note: Persons of Hispanic origin can be of any race.

Source: U.S. Department of Health and Human Services, National Center for Health Statistics.

Table C2.

**Children Reported to Child Protective Services as Alleged Victims
of Child Abuse and Neglect, 1976–1994**

Year	Number of Children	Rate*
1976	669,000	10
1977	838,000	13
1978	836,000	13
1979	988,000	15
1980	1,154,000	18
1981	1,225,000	19
1982	1,262,000	20
1983	1,477,000	24
1984	1,727,000	27
1985	1,928,000	31
1986	2,086,000	33
1987	2,178,000	34
1988	2,265,000	35
1989	2,435,000	38
1990	2,577,645	41
1991	2,695,658	41
1992	2,922,513	43
1993	2,936,554	43
1994	2,935,470	43

*Reported cases per 1,000 children in the population.

Source: U.S. Department of Health and Human Services, National Center on Child Abuse and Neglect.

Table C3.

Maternal Labor Force Participation of Marrried Women with Children Under Age 6, Selected Years, 1948–1994

| | In the labor force | |
	Number	Percent
1948	1,226,000	10.8
1950	1,399,000	11.9
1955	2,012,000	16.2
1960	2,474,000	18.6
1965	3,117,000	23.2
1970	3,914,000	30.3
1975	4,518,000	36.7
1980	5,227,000	45.1
1985	6,406,000	53.4
1990	7,247,000	58.9
1994	7,723,000	61.7

Source: U.S. Department of Labor, Bureau of Labor Statistics.

Index